I0161633

Simply TASTY

LINDA HAYES

Easy Meals on a Budget

Simply Tasty

Easy Meals on a Budget

By: Linda Hayes

©2013, Linda Hayes

Moreno Valley, CA

ISBN: 978-0-9885453-3-5 Hard Cover

ISBN: 978-0-9885453-4-2 Paperback

All rights reserved. This book may not be reproduced in whole or in part, or stored in or introduced into a retrieval system, or transmitted in any form or by any means, electronic, mechanical, photocopying, recording, scanning, or otherwise without prior written permission of the author. The scanning, uploading, and distribution of this book via internet or via any other means without the permission of the author is illegal and punishable by law.

Facebook Page: www.facebook.com/heartchatter

Author Site: www.HeartChatter.com

Published by: Publishing USA www.Publishing-USA.com

DEDICATION

This book is dedicated to my family, extended family, and friends. The art of cooking comes as a long journey of learning, experimenting, sharing ideas, and passing on family traditions. I dedicate this to all my children and especially Marine who birthed the idea of a family cookbook for us to use and our future generations to enjoy.

I dedicate this book to all my readers as they taste and enjoy a piece of our family heritage in the recipes that follow.

INTRODUCTION

The art of cooking and sitting down together as a family sharing a meal is sometimes a fond memory and not part of our busy lives today. I have noticed that when we meet friends the common phrase is "Let's do lunch." Eating together is a special way to break down barriers, get to know each other in a relaxed setting, and develop relationships.

This informative cookbook includes dishes from around he world. You will sample traditional American, Soul Food, Italian, Mexican, Chinese, Filipino, and Thai tasty foods. The recipes were created to be easy to make and budget friendly. More importantly you will make tasty and scrumptious meals that are memorable. Can you imagine people saying "Wow, how did you make that...this is delicious!"

I learned to cook by reading recipes and watching my family and friends cook. We did not measure in the traditional way. Instead, we used pinches and handfuls! I rarely measure today but use kitchen spoons and shakes from the spice bottle when I cook. I have given you close approximates in the ingredient list. I suggest that you add or subtract spices according to your taste. Also, I encourage you to use what you have in your pantry and learn to substitute. If you don't have an ingredient in your recipe try to use what you do have that is similar. Experiment and be creative!

Cooking is a creative art. My cookbook will give you the basic recipes and many variations to spice them up. I encourage you to let your creativity flow as you put your own special touches into the recipes in my cookbook. You will learn how to "cook smart" with my handy tips that can save you time and money.

As a special surprise I included inspirational quotations throughout the book making Simply Tasty part of my Heart Chatter collection. For me, this cookbook is a priceless gift to my family. It will be passed down to my grandchildren and their children. I hope that you will treasure your new favorite recipes and pass them down to your families too.

Enjoy your journey to good food, good health, and joyful living!

Table of Contents

Hints and Tips........................ 1—3

Seasoning Techniques 1

Battering Techniques................ 1

Baking & Cake Tips 2

Basic Spice List......................... 2

General Tips and Hints 3

Appetizers ....4—10

Honie's Hot Wings 6

Spicy Salsa Cheese Dip.............. 6

Fiesta Party Dip 7

The Best Salsa 7

Honie's Guacamole................... 7

Nutty Cheese Ball 8

Cream Cheese Fruit Dip 8

Creamy Lemon Dip 8

Kids Fun Food ....9—10

Fun Grilled Cheese.................... 9

Peanut Butter Treats 9

Easy Kid's Pizza 9

Kid's Morning Treat 10

Pizza Face Wedge 10

Funny Face Pizza...................... 10

Ground Beef ....11—20

Zucchini and Meatballs............ 12

Tin Nok Tok 12

Cabbage Rolls.......................... 13

Stuffed Peppers....................... 13

Spaghetti Sauce....................... 14

Marinara Sauce 14

Taco Casserole 14

Lasagna................................... 15

Vegetable Lasagna 15

Bean & Beef Casserole............. 16

Easy Beefy Noodles 16

Chili Mac................................. 17

BBQ Style Mac......................... 17

Mexican Style Mac 17

Chili with Beans....................... 18

Spanish Tortilla Pie.................. 18

Meatloaf 19

Beef...................................21—26

Corned Beef Hash.................... 22

Chicken Fried Steak 22

Seasoned Cube Steak 22

Smothered Steak..................... 23

Swiss Steak.............................. 23

Steak and Glazed Onions 23

Crock Pot Beef Stew 24

Shepherds Pie 24

Oxtail Stew.............................. 25

Pot Roast 26

Pork...................................27—29

Baked Ham.............................. 28

Country Style Ribs 28

Table of Contents

Pork Cont. ....27—29

Pork Chops 29

Breaded Pork Chops 29

Pork Ribs 29

Spanish Pork Chops 29

Seafood ....30—34

Baked Salmon........................ 32

Italian Baked Fish 32

Fried Fish & Shrimp 32

Pan Fried Fish........................ 32

Tuna Casserole 33

Cheesy Tuna Casserole 33

Shrimp in Wine Sauce............. 33

Croquettes 34

Meatless Meals ....35—38

Chili Rellano 36

Chili Rellano Casserole............ 37

Enchiladas 37

Eggplant Parmesan................. 38

Black Beans and Rice 38

Vegetarian Tortilla Pie 38

Vegetable Stir Fry 38

Poultry ....39—48

Chicken Toast........................ 40

Oven BBQ Chicken.................. 40

Smothered Turkey Wings......... 41

Fajitas 41

Chicken Cacciatore 42

Cornish Game Hens................. 43

Chicken and Vegetables........... 44

Stuffed Chicken Breast 44

Roasted Turkey 45

Roasted Chicken..................... 46

Shredded Chicken 46

Chicken in Green Sauce 46

Chicken Tacos 46

Chicken Casserole 46

Fried Chicken 47

Smothered Chicken 48

Chicken Parmesan................... 48

Soups ....49—52

Chicken Soup......................... 50

Split Pea Soup 50

Navy Bean Soup 51

Cheddar Potato Soup 51

Chinese Noodle Soup 51

Chicken Tortilla Soup.............. 52

Lentil Soup 52

Beans ....53—55

Basic Beans 54

White Beans........................... 54

Black Beans........................... 54

Black Eyed Peas...................... 54

Lentils 55

Table of Contents

Beans Cont. ....53—55

Mongo (Mung) Beans 55

Baked Beans 55

Asian Dishes ....56—63

Lumpia (Filipino Egg Roll).........58

Lumpia 2 58

Egg Foo Yong.........................59

Tempura 59

Basic Chow Mein 60

Chicken Chow Mein...............60

Basic Stir Fry...........................61

Chicken Teriyaki 62

Pancit Bihon 62

Adobo 63

Pad Thai 63

Side Dishes ....64—76

Stuffing...................................66

Fried Rice 67

Spanish Rice 67

Easy Refried Beans 68

Scalloped Potatoes 68

Fried Green Tomatoes.............68

Potato Patties..........................69

Home Fried Potatoes..............69

Twice Baked Potatoes..............70

Fried Cabbage 70

Sautéed Zucchini 71

Green Beans...........................71

Greens 72

Stuffed Zucchini......................73

Candied Yams.........................73

Whipped Yams 74

Potato Salad...........................74

Mac & Cheese/Stove Top 75

Mac & Cheese Baked #1 75

Mac & Cheese Baked #2 76

Greek Vegetables 76

Salads...............................77—81

Seafood Salad 78

Cucumber Salad 78

Fruit Salad..............................78

Pasta Salad.............................79

Ham Salad..............................79

Chicken Salad 79

Shrimp Salad 79

Italian Pasta Salad 80

Seafood Pasta Salad 80

Three Bean Salad....................80

Coleslaw.................................81

Waldorf Spring Salad 81

Summer Fruit Salad 81

Breakfast...........................82—86

Huevos Rancheros...................84

Honie's Easy Donuts 84

Table of Contents

Breakfast Cont. ....82—86

French Toast—Traditional........ 85

French Toast Pastry 85

Basic Omelet 86

Jazzed Up Pancakes 86

Breakfast Potato Hash 86

Sauces and Batters ....87—89

Brown Gravy 88

Turkey Gravy 88

White Sauce 88

Cheese Sauce 88

Honie's BBQ Sauce 89

Fried Fish Batter 89

Asian Marinade 89

Fish Marinade 89

Desserts & More..............90—101

Berry Topping.......................... 92

Honie's Cake Filling.................. 92

Cream Cheese Frosting............ 92

Whip Cream Frosting............... 93

Whipped Deco Frosting 93

Banana Nut bread 93

Easy Glazes............................. 94

Fudge Frosting......................... 94

Buttercream Frosting............... 94

Decorator Frosting................... 94

Honie's Cheesecake................. 95

Choc. Swirl Cheesecake 95

Graham Cracker Crust 95

Chocolate Cooke Crust 95

Brownies................................. 96

Oatmeal Cookies 96

Chocolate Chip Cookies 97

Peanut Butter Cookies............. 97

Cake Bon Bons 98

Fruit & Pudding Cups............... 98

Strawberry Shortcake.............. 99

Berry Cake Delight................... 99

Fruit and Cake Cups................. 99

Basic Spa Water 100

Spa Water Quencher 100

Spa Water Refresher 100

Tropical Party Punch.............. 100

Easy Party Punch 101

Citrus Party Punch................. 101

Pink Party Punch 101

Flavored Iced Drink 101

Index .... 103—106

Hints and Tips

Seasoning Techniques

♦ Lay your meat out in a pan and liberally sprinkle your seasonings on one side. Turn and do other side. Do not be scared to season your dishes. The liberal seasoning is what makes the dish go from good to *Great!*

♦ Use the seasonings you have in your cabinet...when grilling or cooking meats in the oven mixtures of herbs, herb blends, cajun spices, pepper blends, BBQ blends, garlic, onion, and pepper all work well. Experiment and mix them up. More is better than less.

♦ If you are following a cooking recipe (does not apply to baking) get the general idea from the recipe then put your own touch to it. Add the spices to your taste and adjust the recipe to your preferences. Be creative. For meats, poultry, and fish most seasoning combinations work well together. Think out of the box!

♦ When marinating meats, the longer you marinate the more flavorful the dish will be. If you marinate an item over 15 minutes put it in the refrigerator. Marinating overnight works really well if you have the time.

Battering Techniques

Temperature: Prep time 10 minutes

Ingredients: Flour, beaten egg, batter mix

Directions:

Take your fish, chicken, vegetable, or whatever you want to batter and moisten with water or milk. Dust with flour. Next dip into your egg mixture that is made with a beaten egg with 1 TBS. water mixed in it (**egg wash**). Last dip your food into your batter covering well. Fry or bake according to your recipe.

Use this technique with fried chicken, fish, meats, battered vegetables, or chili rellanos.

Hints and Tips

Coat pie pastries with an egg wash (beaten egg with water) before baking then sprinkle with sugar and bake.

Baking

◆ Baking is very different from cooking techniques. My general style of using a recipe as a guide does not apply to most baking recipes. Baking is a precise science where the chemical reactions between ingredients makes the recipe work correctly.

◆ Follow dry and liquid ingredient amounts as stated. You can add extra spices like cinnamon, vanilla, nutmeg, etc. in small amounts and not ruin the recipe. Always bake at specified temperatures and the times as directed.

◆ You can be creative with uncooked fillings and sauces you use with your baked recipes.

Coating For Cake Pans

Mix equal parts of Crisco shortening and flour. Brush onto your cake pans evenly before baking. When using cake mixes mix for the exact time as listed. First blend all the ingredients on low. Next blend for the required time. Do not over mix.

Basic Spice List

Garlic & onion powder or granules

Dehydrated minced onion and minced garlic

Italian seasoning and oregano

Dried basil & dried parsley

Chicken and steak rubs

Granulated BBQ seasoning for meat and chicken

Celery salt and seasoning salt

Cinnamon powder

Vanilla extract

Ground ginger and ground nutmeg

Baking soda and baking powder

Corn starch

Pepper—ground and course grind

Cajun spice and red pepper flakes

Bouillon—beef and chicken

Dried rosemary and dried thyme

Hints and Tips

- Use the measurements as *guidelines*. Alter them to your taste especially with the spices. I learned to cook by watching. Our measuring spoons were handfuls and pinches. I rarely measure my ingredients except in baking. I have given you approximate measurements in the recipes. You can adjust them.

- Use foil on your pans when cooking oven baked meals when possible—it makes cleanup much easier.

- Cover oven baked dishes such as chicken, roasted whole chicken/turkey, etc. with the aluminum foil shiny side in. The shiny side in will draw the heat to the dish, the shiny side up draws it away creating less heat.

- When using foil to cook turkey and foil pocket dishes make sure it is sealed tightly to keep the steam in and keep it moist. When you open the foil reseal it tightly again. Try to keep the dish sealed as long as possible before opening the foil. The tight seal keeps it moist while it cooks.

- Anywhere I have used dried spices like garlic powder, parsley, or italian seasoning , fresh spices can be substituted.

- Learn to improvise. These recipes were created from cooking on a slim budget using whatever was available at home. If you want an upscale version use fresh and more expensive ingredients such as fresh garlic not granulated. If you do not have an ingredient substitute something else that is similar.

- Buy your basic seasonings and spices from discount stores or Wal-Mart.

- Use ground turkey instead of ground beef. You can also mix half ground beef and half ground turkey.

- Use a crock pot to cook your chili, spaghetti sauce, beans, and bean soups as a time saver when you work.

Appetizers

Hot Wings

Cheese Ball

Guacamole

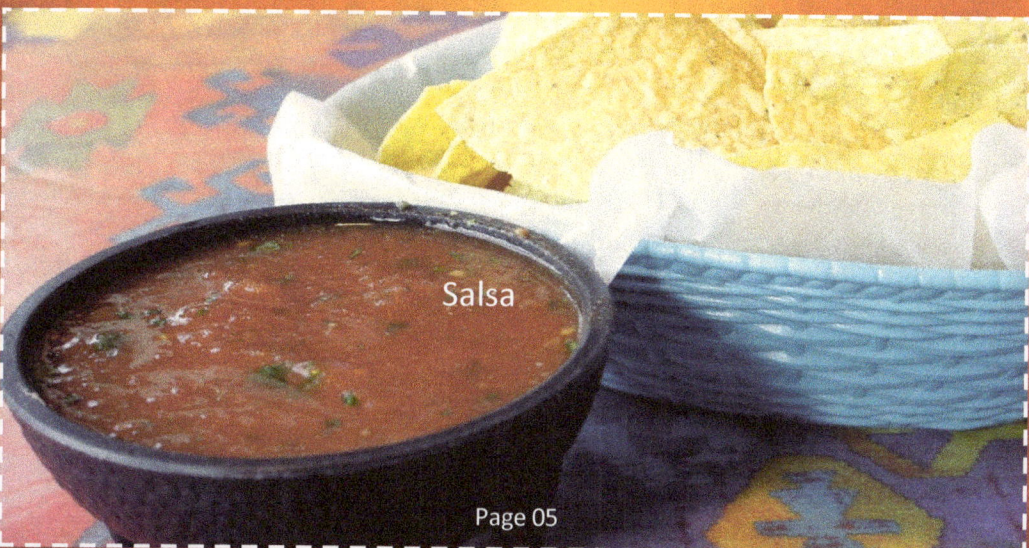
Salsa

Appetizers

Honie's Hot Wings

3 lbs. uncooked chicken hot wing parts

3 tsp. onion powder

3 tsp. garlic powder or granules

1 1/2 tsp. hickory seasoning

3 tsp. cajon spice

1 tsp. pepper

3 tsp. BBQ seasoning or rub

Your favorite BBQ sauce or hot wing sauce

Temperature: Oven 375 degrees for 1 1/2 hours Serves 4—5

Directions:

Take chicken pieces and sprinkle seasonings on both sides of the wing pieces. Be liberal with your seasonings. Line a baking pan with foil and place the wings on it. Cook half way through until the first side browns. Drain any liquid that has filled the pan then turn the chicken over. Continue cooking until done.

Dip chicken pieces in sauce and return to oven for 10 minutes. If you like the wings browned place in your broiler for a few minutes to brown.

Grill Recipe:

Grill wings until done—about 45 minutes. Coat the wings with the sauce and place in oven broiler for a few minutes to brown.

Spicy Salsa Cheese Dip

8 oz. pkg. cream cheese

1 small jar salsa

1/4 cup chopped green onions or chives

Prep time 10 minutes

Directions:

Soften cream cheese to room temperature. Gently mash the cheese to get rid of the rectangular shape. Do not whip it. Pour salsa on top. Top with green onions if desired.

Variations:

Add chopped olives. Add a layer of sour cream on top of cream cheese. Add some finely chopped jalapeño peppers. Serve with tortilla chips.

Recipe For Love

You cannot really love someone else until you learn self-love...

Learn to love yourself first...

Once you do love will flow from you to others you meet and people in your life...

"A journey of a thousand miles begins with a single step." Lao Tzu

Appetizers

Fiesta Party Dip

1 large can refried beans

1 jar salsa

1 pint sour cream

1 1/2 cups guacamole

Sliced olives

2 cups shredded cheddar/jack cheese

1/2—3/4 cups chopped green onions

1/2 tsp. garlic powder

1 tsp. onion powder

Prep time 15 minutes   Serves 6—7

Directions:

Take beans and add garlic and onion powder. Mix well. Take a large baking pan or casserole (square or rectangular if possible) and spread out refried beans across the bottom.

Spread sour cream across the beans for the next layer. Add the guacamole. Top with salsa. Sprinkle cheese across the top and then the olives and green onions. Refrigerate and serve cold with tortilla chips.

The Best Salsa

1 16 oz. can tomatoes

2 jalapenos (mild) or 3 for hot

3 yellow chilies

1 lemon juiced

1/2 medium onion

1 small bunch cilantro

Salt & pepper to taste

Garlic granules to taste

Prep time 10 min.—Makes 5 cups

Directions:

Remove seeds from the peppers. Cut vegetables in large chunks for blender. Add all ingredients except spices and blend on high until it reaches a saucy consistency. Add 3/4 tsp. garlic to start and salt and pepper to taste. If it needs more seasoning add to it. If it is too hot add more tomatoes. If it is not hot enough add another jalapeño and blend again. The finished consistency should be very finely chopped and saucy with no large chunks. For a hotter sauce add 1—2 serrano chilies to the recipe.

Variation:

Use 5 ripe roma tomatoes instead of canned tomatoes.

Honie's Guacamole

3 ripe avocados mashed

1/4 cup salsa

2 tsp. mayonnaise

1/4 cup diced tomatoes

1/4 cup diced onions

Lemon wedge

Garlic, salt, and pepper to taste

Add mashed avocados, mayo, salsa, and vegetables and mix together with a fork. Add 1/4 tsp. garlic powder. Add salt and pepper to taste. Squeeze juice from 1 small lemon wedge into mixture to keep it from turning brown. Mix well.

Appetizers

Cheese Ball

1 pkg. cream cheese

8 oz. shredded cheddar cheese

8 oz. jack or jalapeño jack cheese shredded

1/2 cup chopped green onions or chives

1 pkg. sour cream & chives dip mix or 1/2 pkg. dry onion soup mix

1/2 tsp. garlic powder

1/2 tsp. paprika

Prep time 15 minutes

Directions:

Soften cream cheese to room temperature. Mix the cheeses together in a bowl. Add spices and mix well. Use an electric mixer if available. Form the mixture into a ball with your hands. Roll the ball in the green onions. You may use 1/3 cup chopped nuts with or instead of the green onion. Place on waxed paper and chill.

Variations:

Roll in seasoned toasted almonds, crunchy onion salad topping, or crunchy french onion topping.

Serve with vegetables and crackers.

Cream Cheese Fruit Dip

1 8 oz. pkg. cream cheese

1 tsp. vanilla extract

3/4 cup brown sugar

1/4 cup powdered sugar

1 TBS. milk

Prep time 10 minutes

Directions:

Soften cream cheese to room temperature. Whip with an electric mixer until creamy. Add the sugars and beat until well mixed and fluffy. Stir in vanilla and milk. Mix well and chill.

Serve with cut fresh fruit.

Creamy Lemon Dip

1 8 oz. pkg. cream cheese

8 oz. vanilla yogurt

1 1/4 TBS. lemon juice

1/8 cup pineapple juice

1 tsp. vanilla extract

1 cup powdered sugar

Prep time 10 minutes

Directions:

Follow directions for Cream Cheese Fruit Dip except beat the cream cheese and yogurt together. Follow the rest of the recipe as directed. Chill and serve with fresh fruit.

"The successful person has unusual skill at dealing with conflict and ensuring the best outcome for all." Sun Tzu

Fun Grilled Cheese

Bread, bagel, or english muffin

Sliced cheese

Ketchup

Temperature: Broiler

Directions:

Lightly toast a slice of bread, bagel, or english muffin. Place cheese on top. Make a face with two eyes, a dot nose, and a smile on top of cheese using ketchup. Broil until melted.

Peanut Butter Treat

Bread

Peanut butter

Jelly

Raisins

Spread peanut butter on one slice of bread. You can add jelly if you like. Make a face with raisin eyes, nose, and mouth. Cranraisins or other small food items work too. You can also make the smile with banana pieces.

Easy Kid's Pizza

4—6 french bread rolls

1 16 oz. jar or can pizza sauce

2 cups shredded mozzarella cheese

Garlic spread or garlic butter

Sliced pepperoni

Temperature: Oven 400 degrees for 12—15 minutes Serves 4—6

Directions:

Cut the rolls in half the long way (if they are not already precut). Spread a thin layer of garlic spread on each roll. You can make your own garlic spread by mixing butter or margarine with garlic powder or fresh minced garlic. Spread pizza sauce on top of roll. Cover with cheese and add pepperoni. Bake until cheese is melted and mini pizzas are hot.

Variation:

Use english muffins instead of french bread.

Make a funny face as directed in the Pizza Face Wedge recipe.

"Every child is an artist. The problem is how to remain an artist once we grow up." Pablo Picasso

Happy Snacks

Kid's Morning Treat

Your favorite hot cereal

Jelly

Directions:

Make your child's favorite hot cereal. Take 2 TBS. jelly and heat in microwave for 10 sec. or until it is runny. Make a happy face by taking a spoon and dripping the jelly glaze into two eyes and a smile.

Pizza Face Wedge

Cheese pizza—wedge cut

Bell pepper slices

Sliced black olives

Temperature: Cook as directed for pizza

Directions:

Place two pepperoni eyes on each pizza wedge. Add a bell pepper square for the nose. Cut a bell pepper slice for the smile. Put on wedge. Bake as directed on pizza box.

Funny Face Pizza

1 individual cheese pizza

Peperoni slices

Sliced deli ham

Sliced black olives

Temperature: Cook as directed for pizza

Directions:

Take the frozen pizza and make a face with pepperoni eyes. Take the ham and cut a smile and 2—3 inch strips for the hair. Place on pizza. Cut 2 small circles from the ham for the eye pupils. Place on top of the pepperoni. Add a sliced olive on top of the ham circle. Make the nose and ears with slices of bell pepper. Bake as directed.

Ground Beef

Spaghetti Sauce

Taco Casserole

Green Bean and Beef
Casserole

Lasagna

Ground Beef

Zucchini & Meatballs

3—4 large zucchini squash

1 lb. ground beef

2 TBS. olive oil or canola oil

1/2 diced onion

1 8 oz. can tomato sauce

1/2—3/4 can water (use tomato sauce can)

Pepper, garlic, seasoning salt to taste

Temperature: Stove top for 30 minutes
Serves 4—6

Directions:

Make meatballs and brown in large pan. Sauté zucchini slices and chopped onions in olive oil over medium high heat. Stir constantly until squash starts getting soft and translucent. Add seasonings, meatballs, tomato sauce, and water. Cover and simmer about 20—30 minutes until done.

Serve over rice.

Variations:

Use crumbled ground meat instead of meatballs.

Use ground turkey instead of ground beef.

Tin Nok Tok—Beef & Vegetables

1 lb. ground beef

1/2 medium onion diced

2—3 large potatoes diced

1 tsp. garlic powder or granules

1/2 tsp. seasoning salt

1 TBS. beef bouillon

1/2—3/4 tsp. pepper

Water to top of mixture

Temperature: Stove top for 30 minutes
Serves 4—6

Directions:

Brown meat and onions with seasonings in large pot then drain well. Add water, bouillon, and potatoes and let simmer covered for 20—30 minutes until potatoes are tender.

Serve over rice.

Variations:

Add 1 16 oz. can green beans to mixture.

Add 1/2 cup sliced mushrooms.

You can use ground turkey instead of beef.

"Go confidently in the direction of your dreams. Live the life you have imagined." Henry David Thoreau

Ground Beef

Cabbage Rolls

1 lb. meat loaf mix

8 whole cabbage leaves

12 oz. can tomato sauce

1/3 cup water

Salt and pepper to taste

1/4 tsp. onion and garlic powder

Temperature: Stove top for 45 minutes
Serves 4—6

Directions:

Cut off 8 large cabbage leaves. Blanch (wilt) in boiling water for 3—4 minutes. Lay out leaves and stuff with meatloaf mix. Roll up like a burrito and secure the roll with a toothpick to keep it from opening. Put into a large pan and cover with sauce. Season with salt, pepper, onion, and garlic to taste. Add water, cover, and simmer over low heat until cabbage is cooked and the meat is done.

Serve over rice, garlic mashed potatoes, or cheesy pasta.

Stuffed Peppers

1 lb. meat loaf mix

4 large green bell peppers

Ketchup

Temperature: 350 oven for 35—45 minutes   Serves 4

Directions:

Remove top part of the bell pepper. Remove the seeds. Do not cut the sides of the peppers. Stuff pepper with meatloaf mix. Top with ketchup. Bake until done. The meat will be cooked and the peppers soft.

Variations:

Stuff pepper with uncooked ground beef seasoned with garlic, seasoning salt, onion powder, and pepper. Mix meat with 1 cup cooked rice, diced onions and mushrooms and stuff the mixture into the peppers. Bake as directed.

Stuff with ingredients above but do not add the meat. Use chicken or beef flavored rice. Add diced zucchini, tomatoes, and corn.

Ground Beef

Spaghetti Sauce

1 1/2 lbs. ground beef

1 medium onion coarsely diced

1/2 bell pepper coarsely diced

1/2 cup cut mushrooms

1 large can crushed tomatoes (1 lb. 13 oz.)

1 8 oz. can tomato sauce

1 6 oz. can tomato paste

8—12 oz. of water

1 pkg. spaghetti seasoning mix

1 TBS. italian seasoning

2 tsp. garlic powder or granules

1 1/2 tsp. basil

1 tsp. pepper

1/8 tsp. cinnamon

Temperature: Stove top for 3—4 hours
Serves 6

Directions:

Put onions, bell peppers, and mush-rooms in a food processor and blend until very finely chopped. You can add 1/4 cup water to make it blend easier. Brown meat and drain. In a large pot add the vegetable mixture, meat, tomatoes, tomato paste, tomato sauce, water, and seasonings.

Let simmer covered over low heat for two or three hours. Stir every 20—30 minutes. Add more water during cooking as needed.

Marinara Sauce

Follow recipe for spaghetti sauce. Omit the meat and the cinnamon. Increase tomato sauce to 12—16 oz. Cook on low for 1 1/2 - 2 hours.

Taco Casserole

1 10 oz. can refried beans

1 can creamed corn

1 pint sour cream

1 lb. ground beef

1 pkg. taco seasoning

1 pkg. Jiffy corn bread mix

3/4 cup shredded cheddar cheese

1 tsp. garlic powder or granules

1 tsp. onion powder

Temperature: Oven at 350 degrees for 25—35 minutes   Serves 6

Directions:

Brown meat, drain, and add taco seasoning as directed. Mix spices into refried beans. Use a rectangular baking pan or oval casserole dish and add the refried beans and meat. Next make a layer with the corn. Put the sour cream on top. The last layer is the corn bread mix made as directed on the box. Top with cheese and bake until golden brown and the corn bread is cooked.

"Kindness in words creates confidence. Kindness in thinking creates profoundness. Kindness in giving creates love."   Lao Tzu

Ground Beef

Vegetarian Lasagna

1 batch marinara sauce

3/4 pkg. lasagna noodles

1 pt. ricotta cheese

2 lbs. mozzarella cheese shredded

8 oz. parmesan cheese shredded

3/4 cup finely diced zucchini

3/4 cup diced mushrooms

3/4 cup peeled diced eggplant

3/4 cup diced onions

1/2 cup diced bell peppers

1/2 cup shredded carrots

3/4 cup cooked chopped spinach

Temperature: Oven 375 degrees for 40 minutes covered with foil. Remove foil and bake 5 minutes more. Serves 6—7

Directions:

Mix the vegetables together. Assemble as for regular lasagna. Add some of the vegetable mixture with each layer. Add additional cheese if desired.

Lasagna

1 batch spaghetti sauce

3/4 pkg. lasagna noodles

1 pt. ricotta cheese

1 1/2 lbs. mozzarella cheese shredded

8 oz. parmesan cheese shredded

Temperature: Oven 350 degrees for 25—30 minutes   Serves 6

Directions:

Cook lasagna noodles and drain. Line a rectangular pan with foil. Make first layer with noodles completely covering bottom of pan. Spread spaghetti sauce over noodles. Spread 2—3 TBS. ricotta cheese on top of sauce. Cover layer with shredded mozzarella cheese and parmesan cheese. Repeat layers until pan is full. Top layer should be noodles, sauce, and cheese only. Bake until hot and cheese is melted.

" Holding on to anger is like grasping a hot coal with the intent of throwing it at someone else; you are the one who gets burned. " Buddha

Ground Beef

Savory Green Bean & Beef Casserole

1 lb. ground beef

1/2 small onion diced

1 pkg. dry onion soup mix

1 can green beans or 1 cup frozen green beans cooked

3 cups mashed potatoes

3/4 cup shredded cheddar cheese

1/4 cup seasoned bread crumbs

1 tsp. pepper

1 tsp. garlic granules or powder

2 tsp. beef bouillon

Temperature: Oven 350 degrees for 25—30 minutes   Serves 4—6

Directions:

Brown meat and onions with pepper and then drain well. Add onion soup mix, spices, and canned green beans— do not drain. Add a little water if needed. If you are using cooked frozen green beans add 1/2 to 3/4 cup water to mixture. Mixture should be moist and a little saucy. Put mixture in to a baking pan. Spread mashed potatoes over beef mixture. Make sure the potatoes completely cover the dish. Sprinkle cheddar cheese across the top. Sprinkle bread crumb on top of cheese. Bake until hot and top is golden brown and cheese is melted.

Easy Beefy Noodles

1 lb. ground beef

1/2 tsp. garlic powder or granules

1 tsp. seasoning salt

1 tsp. pepper

1 small onion diced

1/2 cup chopped celery

1/2 cup shredded carrots

3/4 cup sliced mushrooms

1/2 cup cooked frozen peas

4 pkgs. Top Ramen soup noodles

Temperature: Stove top for 15 minutes
Serves 4—6

Directions:

Make ramen noodles as directed on package but do not cook them until soft. Make sure they are still hard and undercooked. Do not use the seasoning package yet. Drain and run under cold water to stop the cooking process. Brown meat, onions, mushrooms, celery, and carrots in large skillet then drain well. Make sure the vegetables are cooked. Add seasonings. Add the noodles, peas, and ramen seasoning packages to the meat mixture. Stir thoroughly to mix in the seasoning and meat with the noodles.

Variation:

Use chinese fresh or dry thin egg noodles instead of Top Ramen.

"Painting is poetry that is seen rather than felt, and poetry is painting that is felt rather than seen." *Leonardo da Vinci*

Ground Beef

Variations:

BBQ Style Mac

Add 1/4 cup BBQ sauce to meat mixture and use 1/2 pkg. of chili seasoning for a BBQ tasting dish.

Mexican Style Mac

Omit chili seasoning and add 1 pkg. of taco seasoning mix. Add 3/4 canned corn and 1 cup canned pinto beans. Sprinkle 1/2—3/4 cup cheddar cheese on top for a Mexican tasting dish.

Chili Mac

1 lb. ground beef

1/2 small onion diced

1/4 cup diced bell pepper

1 pkg. chili seasoning mix

4 oz. tomato sauce

1/2—3/4 cup water

12 oz. pasta—elbow or rotini

Temperature: Stove top for 20 minutes
Serves 4—6

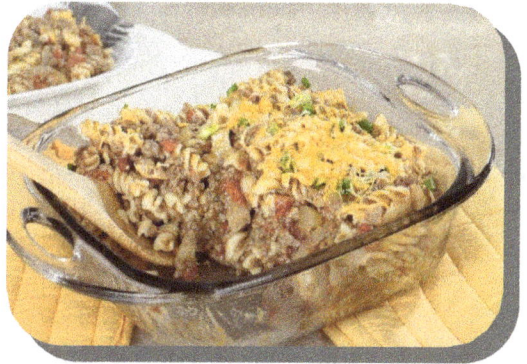

Directions:

Boil pasta until tender, run under cold water, and drain. Brown meat, peppers, and onions in large pan then drain well. Add pepper and salt to taste. Add tomato sauce, water, and chili seasoning package to meat and stir well over medium heat. Let simmer for 10 minutes on low. Add cooked pasta to meat stirring well until it is mixed into the meat mixture. Serve with cornbread, garlic bread, or french bread.

Recipe For Wisdom

Look into your heart...
for within lies the wisdom
you have been seeking...

Ground Beef

Chili with Beans

1 lb. ground beef

1/2 med onion diced

3/4 bell pepper diced

1 jalapeño pepper diced

1 pkg. Chili Seasoning mix (or use boxed chili starter, or brick chili)

1 tsp. chili powder

1 8 oz. can tomato sauce

1 16 oz. can crushed tomatoes

8—12 oz. of water

1 16 oz. can chili beans

1 tsp. garlic powder or granules

1/2—3/4 tsp. pepper

Temperature: Stove top for 30 minutes
Serves 5—6

Directions:

Brown meat, peppers, and onions with garlic, chili powder, and pepper in large pot then drain well. Add tomato sauce, crushed tomatoes, water, chili beans (do not drain) and chili seasoning package to meat and stir well over medium heat. Let simmer on low covered for 25—30 minutes.

Serve with cornbread, garlic bread, or crackers. You may top with shredded cheddar cheese and chopped onions.

Spanish Tortilla Pie

1 lb. ground beef

1/2 medium onion diced

1 pkg. frozen chopped spinach

1 cup diced mushrooms

1/2 cup diced bell peppers

1/2 cup cooked diced potatoes

5—6 eggs beaten

3/4 tsp. garlic and onion powder

1 tsp. seasoning salt

1 tsp. black pepper

Temperature: Stove top for 25 minutes
Serves 4—5

Directions:

Brown beef with all seasonings and vegetables on medium high heat. Drain well. Add cooked potatoes. Squeeze moisture from spinach, chop, and add to mixture. Add eggs then cook on medium low heat covered until the egg is set and almost dry. Remove cover and put a large plate over the pan. Invert the pan so that the tortilla is on the plate. Slide the pie into the skillet cooked side up. Cook until the bottom is golden brown.

Ground Beef

Meatloaf

1 1/2 lbs. ground beef

1 small onion finely diced

1/2 bell pepper finely diced

1 1/2 tsp. garlic powder

1 pkg. onion soup mix

1 tsp. pepper

1 1/2 slices fresh bread

1 egg

1 TBS. water

1/3 cup ketchup

Temperature: Oven 375 degrees for 45 minutes   Serves 5

Directions:

Take the bread and crumble in a food processor. Put raw meat in a large mixing bowl. Add the vegetables, spices, crumbled bread, onion soup mix, ketchup, and egg. Mix together until thoroughly mixed and all the seasonings are incorporated. You need to mix it with your hands. Pack it into a loaf pan pressing it firmly in the pan. Cover with ketchup.

Bake until meat is thoroughly cooked in the middle. Drain off grease after it is cooked.

Other Uses:

Basic meatloaf mix can be used to stuff bell peppers and zucchinis.

You can use the meatloaf mix to bake in mini loaf pans for individual meatloaf portions. Make sure you decrease the cooking time for the mini meatloaf to approximately 30 minutes. Do not overcook.

Recipe for Success

Love can conquer all problems!

Let go of anger...

Let go of ego and the need to be right...

Forget resentment...

Embrace gratitude and joy...

"Do not dwell in the past, do not dream of the future, concentrate the mind on the present moment." Buddha

Beef

Pot Roast

Shepherds Pie

Corned Beef Hash

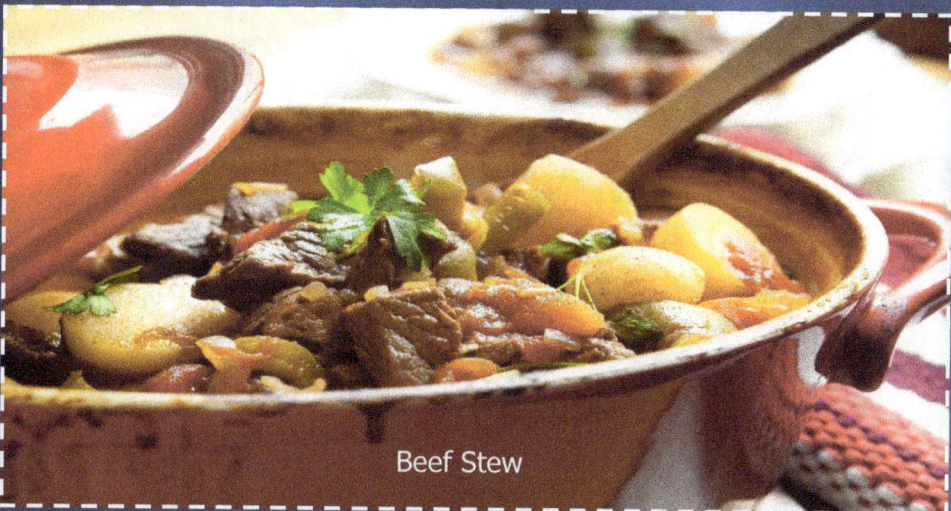
Beef Stew

Beef

Corned Beef Hash

1 can corned beef

3—4 large potatoes diced

1 medium onion finely diced

1/2 bell pepper finely diced

1 1/2 tsp. garlic powder or granules

1 tsp. onion powder

1 tsp. pepper

2—3 TBS. oil

Temperature: Stove top for 15—20 minutes   Serves 4—6

Directions:

Boil potatoes until tender and drain. Add oil, onions, and garlic to a skillet and stir. Add potatoes and cook over medium high heat. When potatoes begin to brown add crumbled corned beef. Season with pepper and salt. Cook until mixture is hot and golden brown on the outside.

Serve with garlic bread, corn bread, or with a fried egg on top of it.

Chicken Fried Steak

1 lb. cubed steak (4 slices)

Canola or vegetable oil for frying

3/4—1 cup flour

1 1/2 tsp. garlic powder

2 tsp. seasoning salt

1 tsp. pepper

1 tsp. onion powder

Temperature: Stove top for 20 minutes

Serves—4

Directions:

Moisten steaks with water. Season with seasonings. Coat each patty well with flour. Deep fry in oil until golden brown and crispy over medium high heat. Serve with brown gravy.

Seasoned Cubed Steak

1 lb. cubed steak (4 slices)

3 TBS. canola or vegetable oil

1 1/2 tsp. garlic powder

2 tsp. seasoning salt

1 tsp. pepper

1 tsp. onion powder

1 cup sliced mushrooms

1 sliced onion

Season the meat with the spices. Pan fry meat until done. Remove from pan. Sauté veggies in oil until soft. Add 2 tsp. soy sauce to them.

"The greatest deception men suffer is from their own opinions."
Leonardo da Vinci

Beef

Smothered Steak

1 1/2 lb. top round steak

2—3 TBS. canola or vegetable oil

1/2 cup flour

1 tsp. garlic powder or granules

1 tsp. seasoning salt

1 tsp. pepper

1 tsp. onion powder

2 tsp. beef bouillon

1/2 onion sliced

1/2 cup sliced mushrooms

1—1 1/2 cups water

2 TBS. flour

Temperature: Stove top for 45—55 minutes   Serves 4

Directions:

Cut steak into 4-6 pieces. Dampen steaks with water. Season with all seasonings except bouillon. Coat each patty well with flour. Brown in oil until brown on each side over medium high heat. Add the rest of the ingredients and stir. Cook over low heat in a covered pan until meat is fork tender. Add more water if needed. The dish will make a gravy as it cooks. Serve with mashed potatoes.

Swiss Steak

Follow the smothered steak recipe but add 1 10 oz. can crushed tomatoes. Add 1/4 cup diced bell peppers.

Steak and Onions

Steak

Seasonings like steak rub or any one you like

1 large onion cut into rings

1 TBS. oil

1 TBS. soy sauce

Temperature: Stove top in cast iron skillet for 20 minutes

Directions:

Heat pan on high until hot. Put steak in pan and lower heat to medium high. Cook on one side until brown; then turn over. Cooking time depends on how you like your steak cooked. You can check the middle of the steak by cutting a small slit with a sharp knife to see if it is cooked to your taste. Take steak from pan. Add 1 TBS. oil, add onions, and sauté on medium high. When the onions are soft add soy sauce. Stir until well coated. You can add 1/2 cup sliced mushrooms if desired.

"Give a man a fish and you feed him for a day. Teach him how to fish and you feed him for a lifetime." Laozi

Beef

Brown all sides of meat. Put meat into crock pot with all the other ingredients. Add seasoning mix and water. Cover and cook on low until vegetables and meat are tender. Check during cooking to see if you need to add more water. Taste to see if you need seasonings. Meat will be fork tender when done.

Variation:

Cook on top of stove for 2—2 1/2 hours on low covered. Add enough extra water to cover meat and vegetables. Dish is cooked when vegetables and meat are tender.

Beef Stew—Crock Pot

1 1/2 lbs. beef stew meat

2 tsp. olive or canola oil

1 large diced onion

1 cup diced celery

1 cup carrots sliced

2—3 large potatoes cut in large chunks

3/4 cup frozen green beans

1 pkg. beef stew seasoning mix

2 tsp. garlic powder or granules

2 tsp. seasoning salt

1/4 tsp. celery salt

1 tsp. pepper

2 1/2 cups—3 cups water

Temperature: Crock Pot on low for 6—7 hours   Serves 5—6

Directions:

Season meat with half the pepper, seasoning salt, celery salt, onion powder, and garlic. Dust with flour then brown meat in oil in a pan.

Shepherds Pie

1 recipe beef stew

3—3 1/2 cups mashed potatoes

1/4 melted butter

1/2 cup seasoned bread crumbs

Temperature: 350 degree oven for 20—30 minutes   Serves 5—6

Directions:

Make the beef stew recipe but do not use potatoes. Pour beef stew into a baking dish. Cover stew with mashed potatoes. Make sure it is completely covered. Pour melted butter and bread crumbs over potatoes. Bake until golden brown.

"The heart has its reasons which reason knows nothing of."
Blaise Pascal

Beef

Oxtail Stew

1 pkg. oxtails

2 tsp. olive or canola oil

1 large can stewed tomatoes

1/2—1 cup water (add as needed during cooking)

1 large onion diced

1 small bell pepper diced

1 cup sliced celery

1 cup sliced carrots or baby carrots

2 large potatoes cut into 8 pieces

1 TBS. beef bullion granulated

2 tsp. garlic powder or granules

3/4—1 TBS. seasoning salt

1—2 tsp. pepper

Temperature: Stove top for 2—3 hours
Serves 4—6

Directions:

Brown oxtails in oil in a large pot. Mix all ingredients into a large pot. Cook over high heat until it comes to a boil. Lower heat to simmer and cover. Cook until meat is tender. Check during cooking to see if you need to add more water. Taste to see if you need more seasonings.

Serve over rice or with corn bread.

Variation:

You can cook this meal in a crock pot on low for 6—8 hours.

Recipe for Happiness

Daily Living—*Live in & enjoy the moment*

Happiness—*Enjoy the journey to the destination. It is the journey that brings happiness*

Love—*Give out love & it will return to you*

Peace—*Cultivate & surround yourself with peace and it will blossom*

Gratitude—*Start each day being grateful and thankful*

Transform Regrets—*Change your regrets into positive life lessons*

Courage—*Recognize your special-ness and let courage flow out of you*

Joy—*Feel the joy of life daily*

Mix each ingredient together daily

and find

ABUNDANT PEACE & JOY

Beef

Pot Roast

1 1/2—2 lbs. thick pot roast

2 tsp. olive or canola oil

Water to cover meat in pot

4 small whole onions peeled

1 cup sliced celery

2 cups whole baby carrots or regular carrots cut in large chunks

6—8 small whole potatoes peeled

2—medium yams quartered

1—2 cups whole green beans cleaned

1 TBS. beef bouillon granulated

2 tsp. garlic powder or granules

1 TBS seasoning salt

2 tsp. pepper

Temperature: Stove Top for 2—2 1/2 hours   Serves 4—6

Directions:

Season meat with pepper, onion powder, and garlic. Dust with flour then brown meat in oil in a large pot. Brown both sides of meat. Mix all ingredients except carrots, potatoes, and string beans in pot. Cook over high heat until it comes to a boil. Heat on low and cover for 45 minutes. Add carrots and potatoes. Add string beans during last 40 minutes of cooking.

Cook 2—3 hours until meat is tender. Check during cooking to see if you need to add more water. Taste to see if you need more seasonings. Meat will be fork tender when done. Serve with rice or garlic/parsley flavored pasta.

Variation:

The dish can be cooked in a meal in a bag pouch in the oven. If you use this recipe brown the meat then add the meat and all the ingredients into the bag. Bake according to the bag directions.

Recipe for Health

Laugh so hard that you cry

A smile instead of a frown

See the positive not the negative

Watch your health and spirit improve daily!

"It is better to remain silent and be thought a fool than to open one's mouth and remove all doubt."   *Mark Twain*

Pork

Pork Ribs

Pork Chops

Breaded Pork
Chops

Baked Ham

Pork

Baked Ham

1 ham (fully cooked, butt portion preferred)

1 can pineapple slices

2 cups brown sugar

1/2 small can frozen orange juice defrosted

1/3 cup pineapple syrup from the canned pineapple

Temperature: Oven at 325—350 degrees. Cook ham 5—7 minutes per pound

Directions:

Mix sugar and orange juice in a bowl. Rub 1/2 of the mixture all over the outside of the ham. Put the pineapple slices on the top of the ham. Attach with toothpicks. Bake ham uncovered. Half way through the cooking add the rest of the glaze on the ham by drizzling it on the ham with a spoon.

Baste the ham often with the glaze drippings as it cooks. This will give you a well glazed and flavorful ham. Ham will be well glazed all over when the cooking time is over.

Variation:

Cut the whole ham into 1/4 inch slices. Pour the glaze ingredients on top of ham slices in a baking pan. Use pineapple chunks instead of slices. Bake for 30 minutes at 350 degrees covered with foil. Baste often and continue cooking until ham is hot and well glazed.

Country Style Ribs

6—8 strips boneless country style pork ribs

Honie's BBQ sauce

2 tsp. garlic powder or granules

1 1/2 tsp. pepper

3 tsp. rib spice

Temperature: Oven at 275—300 degrees for approximately 2—2 1/2 hours Serves 5—6

Directions:

Cut any excess fat of the rib slices. Coat with seasonings. Spread a very thin layer of BBQ sauce on ribs. Put in pan covered with foil. Let cook in oven for 1 hour. Pour off any fat from pan. Continue cooking until fork tender. Uncover ribs the last 20 minutes of cooking and coat with lots of BBQ sauce.

"Some cause happiness wherever they go; others whenever they go."
Oscar Wilde

Pork

Pork Chops

4—6 thin cut center cut pork chops

1/2 tsp. garlic powder or granules

1/2 tsp. onion powder

3/4 teaspoon black pepper

1 tsp. seasoning salt

3 TBS. oil

Temperature: Stove top in frying pan for 20—25 minutes   Serves 4

Directions:

Put oil into pan and heat on medium high heat. Season chops. Fry until crispy and brown on one side then turn over. Continue frying second side until golden brown and crispy. Drain well on paper towels.

Variation:

Coat chops in seasoned bread crumbs and bake for 25—30 minutes at 375 degrees.

For a chop that is thick and juicy instead of thin and crispy use regular or thick cut chops. Follow recipe as above. Cook until meat is no longer pink and cooked. Add an extra 10 minutes to the cooking time.

Pork Ribs

1 slab of pork ribs

2 tsp. garlic powder or granules

2 tsp. onion powder

2 tsp. paprika

1 1/2 tsp. cayenne pepper

1 1/2 tsp. black pepper

3 tsp. bottled rib spice

Honie's BBQ sauce

Temperature: Oven at 250—275 degrees for approximately 2 hours.

Directions:

Mix spices together and rub over the ribs. Marinate 3 hours to overnight in the refrigerator. Put in pan and cover with foil. Bake for 2 hours. Remove ribs from oven and continue cooking on your BBQ grill until thoroughly cooked (about 1 1/2 hours) and tender. Put on BBQ sauce during the last 20 minutes of cooking.

Spanish Pork Chops

4—6 pork chops—center cut

1/2 bell pepper diced

1/2 cup diced onions

1 10 oz. can diced tomatoes

1/2—3/4 cup water

1 tsp. garlic granules or powder

Salt and pepper to taste

Follow pork chop recipe but don't use thin cut chops. Brown the chops in oil until lightly browned. Add the rest of the ingredients and cover. Let simmer for 30 minutes until meat is tender. Serve with mashed potatoes, rice, or pasta.

Seafood

Pan Fried Fish

Fried Shrimp

Croquettes

Shrimp in Wine Sauce

Seafood

Baked Salmon

4 pieces fillet salmon

2 TBS. margarine or butter

1 1/2 tsp. diced fresh garlic

1 tsp. onion powder

1 1/2 tsp. parsley

Temperature: 400 degrees in oven for 15—20 minutes   Serves 4

Directions:

Wash fish and put in a foil lined pan or baking dish. Dot with butter. Season with spices and bake in oven until the middle flakes inside. When cooked squeeze fresh lemon on top.

Italian Style Baked Fish

Follow recipe above but eliminate butter. Season and pour italian dressing over the fish and bake.

You can put thinly sliced tomatoes, onion, and bell pepper on top of seasoned fish, put italian dressing then bake covered with foil for 15 minutes. Uncover and cook for 5 more minutes.

Fried Fish & Shrimp

4—5 pieces of fillet fish (not salmon)

Or 20—24 peeled raw shrimp fan cut

Canola or vegetable oil for deep frying

1 egg mixed with 1 TBS. water

Fish batter recipe (page 89)

Temperature: Stove top for 20 minutes Serves 4

Directions:

Dip fish in egg and coat with fish batter. Or remove shrimp shell but not the tail tip. Remove the vein down the back of the shrimp by pulling it or buy deveined and peeled raw shrimp. Cut the shrimp lengthwise from the back but do not cut all the way through. Make sure you only cut 3/4 of the way through the body. Spread the meat apart so the shrimp is flat (fanning). Batter then fry in hot oil until golden and crispy. Drain well.

Pan Fried Fish

Use the spices for baked salmon. You can use salmon, tilapia, catfish, or red snapper fillets in this recipe. Moisten fillets with milk or water. Season then dip in flour. Fry in olive or canola oil using about 3 TBS. oil. Fry until golden brown on one side then cook second side. Season with salt and pepper to taste.

Seafood

Cheesy Tuna Casserole

Mix one package of the cheese seasoning from a box of Kraft Macaroni and Cheese with the ingredients above. You can use the Kraft Macaroni pasta instead of regular pasta if you like.

Shrimps in Wine Sauce

1 3/4 lb. raw shrimps peeled and deveined

3—4 cloves minced fresh garlic

1/2 tsp. parsley

1/3 cup white wine

1—2 TBS. olive oil

1/2 tsp. paprika

1 1/2 TBS. butter of margarine

1/8 cup water

1 tsp. chicken bouillon

Salt and pepper to taste

Temperature: Stove for 12—15 minutes in skillet   Serves 4

Directions:

Heat oil and lightly brown garlic on medium high heat. Add shrimps and paprika and stir for 2 minutes. Add water, wine, and bouillon. Stir until shrimps are orange in color and cooked. This only takes about 3—5 minutes. When cooked remove shrimp from pan. Leave the sauce in the pan. Add butter and cook on high for 3—5 minutes until the sauce has a rich tasty flavor. Add salt and pepper to taste.

Tuna Casserole

1 can tuna packed in water

1 cup frozen peas

1 12 oz. elbow or rotini pasta or 2 boxes Kraft Macaroni and Cheese mix

1/2 soup can of milk

1 can Cream of Mushroom or Cream of Celery soup

1/2 tsp. pepper

1/2—3/4 tsp. garlic powder

3/4—1 TBS. seasoning salt

Temperature: Oven 350 degrees for 25 minutes   Serves 4—6

Directions:

Boil pasta until tender, run under cold water and drain. Add tuna—do not drain. Add Cream of Mushroom or Cream of Celery soup and 1/2 can milk. Add cooked frozen peas. Season with pepper, garlic, and seasoning salt. Pour mixture in a baking pan and top with shredded cheddar or jack cheese. Bake until bubbling and hot.

Seafood

Croquettes

1 can drained tuna or salmon

1 small onion finely diced

3/4 cup celery finely diced

2 cups fresh bread crumbs

1 cup seasoned bread crumbs

2—3 beaten eggs

1/2 tsp. pepper

3/4 tsp. garlic powder or granules

1 1/2 tsp. seasoning salt

Oil for frying

Temperature: Stove top for 25 minutes

Serves 4—5

Directions:

Take fresh bread crumbs, vegetables, seasonings, and eggs and mix in tuna or salmon. Mixture should be moist and hold together well. If it is too dry add another egg.

Make the into fat patties by molding it in your hands. Roll in seasoned bread crumbs. Make sure it is completely coated. The crumbs will stick to the patties if it is moist enough. Fry in hot oil over medium high heat until golden brown and cooked inside. Drain well. Serve with cheese sauce or white sauce.

Hint: Make fresh bread crumbs with sliced bread in a food processor.

White Sauce

Take 1 TBS. butter or margarine and melt in saucepan. Add 1/4 cup flour a little at a time to the butter. Stir it around being careful to get out any lumps. Do not brown the flour. Add 1—1 1/2 cups water gradually while stirring constantly. You can use a wire wisk if you like. Season with pepper, 1/2 tsp. chicken bouillon granules, and salt to taste.

Cheese Sauce

Make the white sauce above. When it is cooked add 1/2 cup shredded cheddar cheese. Mix until melted.

"A terrace nine stories high rises from a handful of earth; A journey of a thousand miles starts from beneath one's feet." Laozi

Meatless Dishes

Vegetarian Spanish Tortilla

Black Beans and Rice

Enchilada

Eggplant Parmesan

Meatless Meals

Chili Rellanos

4 fresh pasilla chilies

1 lb. cube monterey jack cheese

Flour for dusting

1/4 tsp. salt

3 egg whites—beaten until stiff

3 egg yokes—beaten until fluffy

Oil

Sauce:

1 small jalapeno pepper diced

4 roma tomatoes diced

1/2 onion diced

Oil

3 —4 cloves finely diced garlic

1 cup water

1 TBS. chicken bouillon

Temperature: Prep and cooking time 40 minutes   Serves 4

Directions:

Burn the skins of the peppers on your stove top until they are black and charred. To do this place them on top of your gas burners on high heat. Turn to burn all sides evenly.

Hint: When you choose your peppers try to find large flat ones with fewer ridges for easier charring.

Put the charred peppers in a brown paper sack or plastic bag and seal tight.

Let sit to steam for 15 minutes. Cut the cheese into long strips to fit into the peppers. Run peppers under cold water to make it easier to peel off the blackened skin. Cut a small slit neat the top of the pepper and remove the seeds. Stuff the peppers with the strips of cheese and fold the flesh back on top of the cheese. Dust with flour and set aside. Beat the egg whites until stiff. Beat the egg yolks, salt, and baking powder until light and fluffy. Gently pour the egg yolks into the egg whites and fold carefully. Dip the chilies into the batter and fry until crispy in hot oil. Drain well.

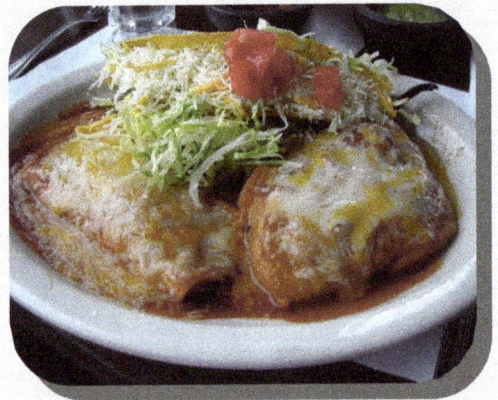

Sauce:

Sauté all the ingredients until the vegetables are soft and mushy. Add water and simmer until the sauce is cooked. Add salt to taste

"The man of virtue makes the difficulty to be overcome his first business, and success only a subsequent consideration." Confucius

Meatless Meals

Chili Rellano Casserole

6 eggs

2 cans (7 oz. each) whole chilies

1 1/4 cups milk

1/2 lb. shredded jack cheese

1/2 lb. shredded cheddar

1 tsp. garlic powder

1/2 tsp. onion powder

1/2 tsp. chili powder

1 TBS. flour

1/4 cup finely chopped onions

1/4 tsp. salt

1/2 tsp. pepper

8 oz. red or green enchilada sauce

Temperature: Oven 350 degrees for 45—50 minutes   Serves 4—6

Directions:

Mix eggs, flour, seasonings and beat with a fork to combine. Grease a rectangular or oval baking dish (9x12). Layer drained chili's across the bottom. Sprinkle jack cheese on top of the layer. Pour half of the egg mixture on top. Make another layer as above. Top with shredded cheddar cheese and chopped onions. Bake for 35 minutes and drizzle sauce over dish. Bake until done. The casserole should be firm. Casserole will thicken as it stands.

Variation:

Top with 8 oz. of salsa instead of enchilada sauce.

Enchiladas

12 corn tortillas

1 large can red or green enchilada sauce

1—1 1/2 lb. shredded cheddar or jack cheese

1/2 cup diced onions or three diced green onions

1/4—1/2 cup oil

Temperature: Oven 25—30 minutes at 350 degrees   Serves 4—6

Directions:

Heat oil in pan on medium high. Dip tortillas in oil to soften them. Drain well on a paper towel. Dip tortillas in enchilada sauce then fill with your cheese. Roll up and place in pan. Put in a foil lined baking pan. Pour sauce over rolled enchiladas. Cover with shredded cheese and sprinkle onions or green onions across the top. Bake until cheese is melted and hot.

Variations:

Stuff with shredded beef, ground taco meat, shredded chicken, or shrimp.

Casserole:

Cut 16 tortillas into strips and heat in oil. Drain well. Grease a rectangular casserole pan then put a layer of tortillas on the bottom. Add meat or chicken, then the sauce. Top with cheese. Repeat layers until pan is full. Top with onions. Bake at 350 degrees for 35—45 minutes.

Meatless Meals

Eggplant Parmesan

1 large eggplant

Italian seasoned bread crumbs

1 egg beaten with 1TBS. water

Canola or vegetable oil for frying

1 16 oz. can tomato sauce

1 1/2 lbs. shredded mozzarella cheese

1 1/2 tsp. italian seasoning

1 tsp. garlic powder or granules

Temperature: Oven 350 degrees for 20—25 min.   Serves 5—6

Directions:

Peel and slice eggplant into thin circular slices. Dip eggplant slices in egg and coat with italian bread crumbs. Fry in canola oil until soft inside and golden outside over med high heat. Drain well to remove as much oil as possible. Prepare a square or rectangle baking pan by spraying with non-stick cooking spray. Make first layer with eggplant completely covering bottom of pan. Spread a layer of tomato sauce over eggplant. Sprinkle with garlic powder and italian seasoning. Sprinkle mozzarella cheese on top. Repeat layers until pan is filled. Add shredded parmesan cheese on top layer with the mozzarella if desired.

Black Beans and Rice

2 cups instant brown rice

1 3/4 cup water

1 TBS. chicken bouillon

1 10 oz. can seasoned black beans not drained

1/3 cup diced bell pepper

1/2 cup diced onions

2 tsp. olive oil or canola oil

2 tsp. garlic powder or granules

Temperature: Stove top for 20—25 minutes   Serves 4—5

Directions:

Brown the vegetables in oil in a small pot. Add the remaining ingredients to the pot of rice. Cook covered on low until rice is fluffy.

Vegetarian Spanish Tortilla Pie

See Spanish Tortilla Pie on page 18 for the meat version of this recipe...*then*

Omit the ground beef. Add 1/2 cup diced cooked zucchini, 1/2 cup chopped cooked asparagus, and 3/4 cup mozzarella or jack cheese. Cook as directed in the meat pie recipe.

Vegetable Stir Fry

See Basic Stir Fry on page 61 for the chicken version of this recipe...*then*

Omit chicken and add 1 cup fried tofu for the chicken. Add last when dish is almost cooked. Omit the tofu and just use the vegetables if desired.

Poultry

Chicken Parmesan

Oven BBQ Chicken

Roasted Turkey

Stuffed Chicken Breast

Poultry

Chicken Toast

2 cups diced cooked chicken

1 1/2 TBS. flour

1 1/2 tsp. chicken bouillon

1 TBS. margarine or butter

1 cup water

Pepper to taste

Variation:

Use 1 6 oz. pkg. Buddig sliced Ham or Turkey

Temperature: Stove top on medium heat for 10—15 minutes   Serves 4

Directions:

Melt margarine in medium saucepan over medium heat. Add chicken and gradually add flour while stirring. Add water a little at a time at first while stirring to keep from getting lumpy. Keep adding water until the mixture has a thin-medium consistency gravy. Turn heat to low. Add more water if needed. Add bouillon and pepper to taste. Simmer for 5—8 minutes to make sure the raw flour taste in the gravy has disappeared. Serve over toast, biscuits, noodles, or mashed potatoes. Can be used as a breakfast or dinner dish.

Variation:

Add frozen peas, diced mushrooms, and carrots if desired.

Oven BBQ Chicken

2 lbs. cut up chicken

1 tsp. garlic powder or granules

1 tsp. pepper

1 tsp. BBQ seasoning

1 tsp. onion powder

1 tsp. monterey chicken seasoning or your favorite seasoning

Liquid smoke

BBQ sauce (my recipe or yours)

Temperature: Oven at 400 degrees for 45 minutes   Serves 4—6

Directions:

Remove skin from chicken and wash pieces. Place on a large tray and season both sides with spices. Drip liquid smoke on the pieces. Put chicken in a large baking pan. Cover and cook for 30 minutes. Coat chicken with BBQ sauce and return to oven. Cook uncovered until tender. Add more sauce if needed.

Recipe for Change

Open your mind to possibilities

Step out of your comfort zone

Gather up your courage. Try

something new!

"Laughter is the universal joyous evergreen of life." Abraham Lincoln

Poultry

Smothered Turkey Wings

2 turkey wings or 2 turkey thighs

1 tsp. garlic powder or granules

1 tsp. pepper

1 tsp. seasoning salt

1 tsp. onion powder

1 tsp. chicken bouillon

1 cup diced celery

1/2 cup sliced mushrooms

1/2 onion diced

1 can Cream of Celery soup

1/2 can of water or milk

Temperature: Oven at 375 degrees for 45 minutes   Serves 3—4

Directions:

Place turkey in a foil lined baking dish or pan. Add the vegetables and put all the seasonings on the meat and vegetables. Pour the soup over the mixture then pour the water over all of it. Cover the pan with foil and cook until tender.

Variations:

This can also be cooked in a crock pot on low for 6—8 hours or until tender.

Add 1 cup sliced carrots, two large potatoes cut in 8 pieces, and two small yams cut in thick slices. Use 1 1/2—2 cans of soup and 1 can water.

Fajitas

1 large chicken breast cut in thin strips

2 tsp. olive or canola oil

1 1/2 tsp. garlic powder

1 tsp. onion powder

1 tsp. pepper

Chicken taco seasoning mix

1 green and red bell pepper or 2 green peppers cut in slices

1 large onion cut in slices

Temperature: Stove top for 20 minutes
Serves 4—6

Directions:

Brown chicken in a large skillet with olive oil. Season with garlic, pepper, and onion. Add vegetables and sauté until meat is cooked and vegetables are crispy tender. Add seasoning mix and stir.

Variation:

Use shrimp or beef instead of chicken or use all three at once.

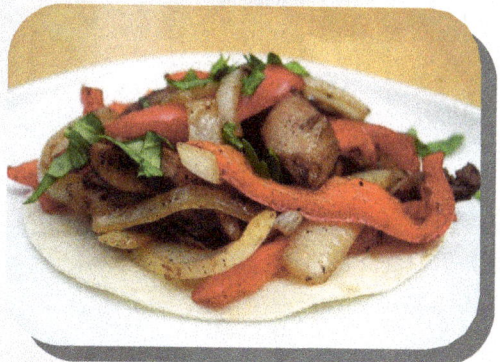

Poultry

Chicken Cacciatore

1 lb. sliced chicken breast

1 small onion coarsely chopped

1/2 bell pepper coarsely chopped

1 16 oz. can crushed tomatoes

1/2 cup of water

1 tsp. italian seasoning

1 tsp. garlic powder or granules

3/4 tsp. pepper

Temperature: Stove top for 45 minutes—1 hour   Serves 4

Directions:

Put onions, peppers, italian seasoning, and tomatoes in a food processor and blend until very finely chopped. Brown chicken pieces seasoned with all the spices. Make sure that the chicken breasts are cut into two or three pieces so they will cook quicker. Drain the oil from chicken in the pan and then add the sauce mixture into the pan with the chicken. Add half of the water. Simmer covered until chicken is tender. Check while it is cooking to see if the dish needs a little more water. Turn the chicken over half way through the cooking process.

Serve with cooked pasta that has been tossed with margarine, garlic, and parsley after it is cooked.

Variation:

You can use chicken thighs if preferred.

You can cut the chicken breasts into chunks instead of large pieces.

Make a chunky sauce by blending the vegetables into a fine texture but leave the tomatoes chunky instead of finely blended.

*"Three things cannot
be hidden:
The sun, the moon,
and the truth."
Buddha*

"A life spent making mistakes is not only more honorable, but more useful than a life spent doing nothing." George Bernard Shaw

Poultry

Cornish Game Hens

2 whole Cornish hens

Chicken rub (garlic, onion, pepper, herbs)

Cooked herbed rice or wild rice mix

1/2 cup chopped celery

1/2 cup chopped onion

1/4 cup chopped mushrooms

1/2 tsp. garlic powder or granules

Glaze:

1/4 cup honey

1/8—1/4 cup pineapple juice

1/2 cup melted butter or margarine

1/4 cup brown sugar

Temperature: Oven 400 degrees for 1—1 1/4 hours   Serves 3—4

Directions:

Remove neck and gizzards from inside the bird cavity. Wash bird inside and out. Sprinkle herb rub inside chicken cavity. Rub the bird on the outside with the chicken herb rub. Stuff inside of bird with your rice mixed with the onions, mushrooms, and celery. Rub the glaze on the outside of the hen. Cook in pan tightly covered with foil. Make sure the foil completely covers pan and is tight. The shiny side of the foil should be inside and the dull side up. This will help draw the heat into the pan. Remove foil from pan the last 15 minutes of cooking.

Chicken is cooked when the inside thigh area juice is clear and not bloody and the meat is tender.

Variation:

Split hen in half down the back side of the bird cutting it lengthwise. Prepare as directed. Add sliced carrots, onions, and potatoes seasoned with garlic, salt, and pepper. Coat veggies with 2 TBS. of olive oil. Bake as directed for 45 minutes.

Recipe for Peace

Be slow to anger…
Be quick to forgive…
Be full of empathy…
Think before you speak…
Judge only yourself…

"The art of being wise is the art of knowing what to overlook."
William James

Poultry

Foil Wrapped Chicken & Vegetables

4 skinless chicken breasts

1 tsp. garlic powder or granules

1 tsp. onion powder

1/2 tsp. pepper

1 tsp. seasoning salt

1 TBS. chicken bouillon

1/2 cup diced celery

2 potatoes cut in quarters

1/2 cup carrots cut in chunks

1/3 cup sliced mushrooms

1/2 onion sliced

Temperature: Oven at 350 degrees for 45 minutes   Serves 4

Directions:

Remove skin from chicken and wash pieces. Place chicken and vegetables in a bowl and sprinkle with all the spices. Take a large piece of foil and put the chicken and vegetables in the middle of it. Close both ends tightly. Fold the top down and close tightly. Bake for 30 minutes. Open the foil and check if it is done. If it needs a little more cooking reseal and cook a little longer.

Variation:

Use ground beef or ground turkey. Dice the potatoes and season the meat. Add yam slices if desired.

Stuffed Chicken Breast

2 chicken breasts

1 tsp. olive or canola oil

1 tsp. garlic powder or granules

1 1/2 tsp. montreal seasoning for chicken or your favorite chicken seasoning blend

1 tsp. pepper

1 box Stove Top stuffing mix

Temperature: Oven 400 degrees for 25—35 minutes   Serves 4

Directions:

Cut each chicken breast into two pieces to make them thinner (do not cut in half cross ways but cut the breast through the entire length. This will give you four thin breasts. Season chicken breast. Prepare stuffing mix according to the directions on the package. Put some of the stuffing on top of the chicken slice then roll the chicken around the stuffing . You can close the roll with a toothpick if needed to keep the stuffing inside the chicken roll. Place on a foil lined pan coated with oil. Bake until chicken is cooked and browned.

Variation:

Stuff with chicken seasoned rice, finely chopped onion, celery, mushrooms, and bell pepper.

Stuff with cooked broccoli, sliced mushrooms, and shredded cheese.

Poultry

Roasted Turkey

Turkey

Oil

Salt

Seasoning (chicken rubs, montreal chicken seasoning, herb rubs)

Temperature: Oven 400 degrees for 3 1/2—4 1/2 hours (13—15 lb. bird)

Directions:

Remove neck and gizzards from inside turkey cavity. Wash bird inside and out. Sprinkle salt inside chicken cavity. Rub olive or canola oil on the outside of bird with your favorite seasoning. Gently insert your hand under the chest skin to loosen it from the bird. Run you hand over the breast and thigh areas loosening the skin. Do not tear it or remove it. Rub seasonings under the skin and let marinate overnight. Rub oil on the outside skin of turkey before cooking. Your bird will have exceptional flavor.

If stuffing turkey stuff the cavity tightly. If you have extra stuffing you can stuff the neck cavity area also. Close cavities with turkey trussing kit. Fold under wings and tie legs. Cook on a rack in a large roasting pan. Make a foil tent

(shiny side of foil inside) to cover the pan tightly covering it. There should be no leaks in the cover. Check the bird after 2 1/4 hours. Make sure you put the foil back tightly. Remove foil from pan the last 15 minutes of cooking. Turkey is cooked when the inside thigh area juices are clear and not bloody and the meat is tender.

Variation:

If you are carving the bird before serving and not presenting it whole try this…

Cut the wings, legs and thighs from the bird before cooking. Cook bird as in recipe. Wrap the wings in a foil tent or pouch Do the same with the legs and thighs. Cook in oven at the same time as the bird. Remove chicken parts after 1—1 1/2 hours when cooked. Your bird will cook faster and the turkey parts will be perfectly cooked. The bird body should cook quicker by 30—45 minutes.

> *"Love is of all passions the strongest, for it attacks simultaneously the head, the heart and the senses."*
> Lau Tzu

"He who knows when he can fight and when he cannot, will be victorious." Sun Tzu

Poultry

Roasted Chicken

1 whole chicken

2 TBS. oil

Chicken rub (garlic, onion, pepper, herbs)

Temperature: Oven 400 degrees for 1—1 1/2 hours   Serves 5—6

Directions:

Follow preparation directions for Roasted Turkey. Chicken is cooked when the thigh area juice is clear and not bloody and the meat is tender.

Variation:

Stuff with stuffing mix, seasoned celery, carrots, and onions or cooked rice with chicken bouillon and mushrooms. Stuffed chicken takes longer to cook— add 20 minutes cooking time.

Shredded Chicken

2 lbs. skinless chicken pieces (breasts or thighs)

1 tsp. garlic powder or granules

3/4 tsp. pepper

2 tsp. seasoning salt

1 tsp. onion powder

Water to cover chicken

Temperature: Stove top for 20—25 minutes

Directions:

Cover chicken with water and spices in a pot and bring to a boil. Cook covered over medium low heat until chicken is tender.

Remove chicken and let cool. Pull the chicken apart to shred the meat. You can also cut it into small pieces for other recipes. Use chicken for pot pies, chicken salad, and the recipes below.

Chicken in Green Sauce

Add cooked chunked chicken to green enchilada sauce and simmer for 8—10 minutes. Use as a filling for chicken enchiladas.

Chicken Tacos

Directions:

Heat diced cooked chicken (or ground beef) in pan and sprinkle some taco seasoning and garlic.

Chicken Casserole

Directions:

Use Tuna Casserole in the Seafood section but substitute 1 can chunked chicken or 1 1/2 cups cooked chunked chicken for tuna. Add frozen carrots and peas if desired.

Poultry

Fried Chicken

12 pieces of chicken

Canola or vegetable oil –to fill the skillet 3/4 way full

1/2 cup flour to dust chicken

2 cups flour for flour mixture

2 eggs mixed with 2 TBS. water

Flour Seasonings:

1 1/2 tsp. garlic powder or granules

1 1/2 tsp. onion powder

1 tsp. paprika

2 1/2 tsp. seasoning salt

2 tsp. cajon spice or 1 1/2 tsp. herb or chicken spice

1 tsp. pepper

Temperature: Stove top for 30—40 minutes   Serves 6

Directions:

Make coating mixture by mixing flour, seasoning salt, pepper, garlic powder, onion powder, paprika, cajon spice or any other special spices or herbs you like. Put oil in skillet and heat on high heat. Wet chicken with water then season chicken pieces with pepper, paprika, garlic powder, and salt. Dip chicken in flour to make a light coat on pieces. Dip chicken in egg wash (egg and water mixture). Dip chicken into flour mixture and coat well covering all parts of the chicken. The coating should be thick and stick to the entire piece of chicken.

Fry in hot oil turning over half way through the cooking time. If the pan is tightly packed with chicken pieces you can leave the chicken on medium high to high heat. If you have fewer pieces of chicken lower heat a little to allow the chicken to cook completely and not brown too quickly. Chicken is done when it is golden brown and no blood comes out of the chicken when you pierce it with a fork. Drain well on paper towels.

"When you have faults,

Do not fear to abandon them"

Confucius

"Laugh and the world laughs with you . Weep and you weep alone."
Ella Wheeler Wilcox

Poultry

Smothered Chicken

6—8 pieces chicken

1/4 cup oil

1 beaten egg & 1/2 cup milk

1 cup flour

1 tsp. paprika

1 1/2 tsps. garlic powder

1 tsp. onion powder

1 tsp. pepper flake mix (sweet peppers not hot peppers)

2 tsp. chicken bouillon

1 tsp. seasoning salt

Pepper to taste

Water (about 1 or 1 1/4 cups)

Temperature: Stove top for 45—60 minutes   Serves 4—6

Directions:

Wash chicken pieces then dip in milk mixture. Lay out flat and season with salt, pepper, and paprika. Mix the flour with the rest of the spices and pepper. Dip the chicken pieces in the flour mix. Coat well on all sides. Brown chicken in hot oil in a large pan browning all sides over medium high heat. Pour out any extra oil leaving about 1 1/2 TBS. in pan with chicken.

Add 2—3 TBS. of flour to the pan and stir it around until it has a crumbly consistency over medium heat. If you have extra flour mix you can use that or just use plain flour. Add water and chicken bouillon to cover the chicken.

Cover and cook over low heat until chicken is tender. Check half way through to see if the sauce has tuned into a flavorful gravy. If the gravy is too thick add water. If it is too thin sprinkle 2 or 3 tsp. of flour into the sauce. Stir constantly to keep it from forming lumps.

Chicken Parmesan

4 thin cut chicken fillets

1 cup seasoned bread crumbs

1 egg with 1 TBS. water

1 tsp. onion powder

1 1/2 tsp. garlic powder

1 tsp. italian seasoning

1 cup marinara sauce

3/4 cup shredded mozzarella cheese

1/2 cup parmesan cheese

Oil

Temperature: Stove top for 15—20 minutes   Serves 4

Directions:

Season chicken then dip in egg wash. Dip in bread crumbs making sure to cover it completely. Fry in hot oil over medium high heat until golden brown. Spread marinara sauce on the chicken and put cheese on top of the sauce. Melt in a 350 degree oven for 10—12 minutes or place in broiler to melt cheese. Serve with pasta.

SOUPS

Chinese Noodle Soup

Navy Bean Soup

Split Pea Soup

Chicken Tortilla Soup

Soups

Chicken Soup

2 lbs. chicken pieces

1 onion diced

1 cup celery diced

1 cup sliced carrots

1 1/2 cups chopped cabbage

1 large zucchini thinly sliced

2 large potatoes diced

(any other vegetable you would like to add)

2—3 TBS. chicken bouillon

1 1/2—2 TBS. seasoning salt

2 tsp. pepper

1 tsp. garlic powder or granules

1/3 cup dried lentils

1/3 cup uncooked rice

1 large pot of water (10—12 cups)

Temperature: Stove top for 1 1/2 hours   Serves 6—8

Directions:

Fill large pot with chicken parts and cover with water. Add pepper and salt. Boil until chicken is tender (about 30 minutes). Remove cooked chicken from broth. Add remaining ingredients to the broth. Cut chicken into bite size pieces and return to broth. Let simmer for 30—45 minutes until the rice, lentils, and vegetables are soft. Add more bouillon and seasoning salt if needed. If you have the leftover bones from a whole turkey or chicken you can boil the carcass in the water for 30—45 minutes to make a chicken stock .

Use in the recipe instead of the water. Make sure you strain the broth before using it in the soup.

Split Pea Soup

1 lb. dried split peas

8 cups water

1 large onion diced

1 cup diced carrots

2 tsp. garlic powder or granules

2 tsp. seasoning salt

1/2 tsp. pepper

Bacon ends, ham bone, or hock

Temperature: Stove top for 1 1/4 hours   Serves 6

Directions:

Mix all ingredients into a large pot. Bring to boil on high. Lower heat to simmer and cover. Cook one hour until peas are soft and mushy. Add more water if needed. If soup is too thin cook on high and let boil for 10 minutes to thicken.

Soups

Navy Bean Soup

1 lb. navy beans

8 cups water

1 large onion diced

1 small bell pepper diced

1 large tomato diced

1/2 cup diced celery

2 tsp. garlic powder or granules

3/4—1 TBS. seasoning salt

1 1/2 tsp. pepper

Bacon ends, ham hock, or ham bone

Temperature: Stove top for 1 1/2—2 hours   Serves 6

Directions:

Mix all ingredients into a large pot. Cook on high until boiling. Lower heat to simmer and cover. Cook until beans are tender and the liquid starts to thicken. Check during cooking to add more water if needed. Add seasonings as needed.

Cheddar Potato Soup

2 TBS. butter or margarine

1/4 cup diced celery

1/2 cup diced onion

1 3/4 cups chicken broth

3 large diced & peeled potatoes

3 TBS. flour

2 1/2 cups milk

1 tsp. black pepper

Salt to taste

2 tsp. fresh parsley or flakes

2 cups grated cheddar cheese

Temperature: Stove top for 30 minutes
Serves 4

Directions:

Melt the butter and cook celery and onions until they are tender. Add chicken stock and potatoes and cook on low until potatoes are soft. Add the rest of the ingredients except the cheese. Stir until flour, milk, and spices are well mixed. Keep stirring until thick. Add cheese and stir until melted. Serve with crumbled cooked bacon and diced chives.

Chinese Noodle Soup

6—8 cups chicken broth

3/4 lb. thinly sliced chicken

1/2 onion cut in chunks

1/2 cup sliced mushrooms

3 stocks bok choy cut up

1/2 cup chopped chinese cabbage

1 TBS. thinly sliced fresh ginger

2 TBS. soy sauce

1/4 lb. rice noodles (Thai type-thin)

Temperature: Stove top for 15 minutes   Serves 4—5

Directions:

Add all ingredients to the pot and bring to a boil on high heat. Lower heat and simmer for 12—15 minutes until noodles are cooked.

Soups

Lentil Soup

1 lb. dried lentils

8 cups water

1 large onion diced

1/2 cup diced carrots

3/4 cup chopped celery

2 tsp. beef bouillon

2 tsp. garlic powder or granules

2 tsp. seasoning salt

1 1/2 tsp. pepper

Bacon ends, ham chunks, or ham bone

Temperature: Stove top for 1 hour
Serves 6

Directions:

Mix all ingredients into a large pot. Heat over high heat until it comes to a boil. Lower heat to simmer and cover. Cook 45 minutes to an hour until beans are soft. Add more water if needed. If soup is too thin cook on high and let boil for 10 minutes to thicken. If it is too thick add more water.

You can use the leftover turkey bones or smoked turkey legs or thighs for the meat as well. Cook longer if using turkey legs or thighs. Cook until turkey is tender.

Chicken Tortilla Soup

1 cup diced onions

3 cloves minced garlic

2 jalapeños seeded and diced

1 diced pasilla chili

2 cups diced fresh tomatoes

1 cup diced carrots

2 tsp. ground cumin

1/2 tsp. ground coriander

1 TBS. tomato paste

1 cup frozen corn

6 cups chicken stock

1 tsp. salt

1 1/2 cups cooked chicken diced

2 TBS. olive or canola oil

Temperature: Stove top for 45 minutes
Serves 4—5

Directions:

Sauté first five ingredients in oil until mushy. Add carrots, tomato paste, spices, and corn and stir for a few minutes. Add chicken stock. Add chicken and simmer for 35—45 minutes. Taste and add more salt and some pepper if needed. You can also add a little chicken bouillon if needed.

Serve with crumbled tortilla chips, shredded jack cheese, and finely chopped fresh cilantro on top of each bowl. Garnish with a lime wedge.

Hint:
Boil your raw chicken in water with garlic, salt, onion powder, and pepper. Strain and use the chicken broth with 2—3 TBS. chicken bouillon and water to make the 6 cups stock needed for the recipe. You can also used canned chicken broth.

Beans

Black Eyed
Peas

White Beans

Baked Beans

Lentils

Beans

Basic Beans

4 cups dried beans (pinto, red, Great Northern White beans, black beans)

8—12 cups water

1 large onion diced

1 small bell pepper diced

2 tsp. garlic powder or granules

1 TBS. seasoning salt

2 tsp. pepper

Seasoning meat (bacon ends, ham chunks, ham hock, smoked turkey leg, neck bones, or ham bone)

Temperature: Stove top for 2—3 hours
Serves 6—8

Directions:

Mix all ingredients into a large pot. Cook over high heat until it comes to a boil. Lower heat to simmer and cover. Cook 2—3 hours until beans are tender and the liquid starts to thicken.

Check during cooking to see if you need to add more water. Taste to see if you need more seasonings. If broth is still watery and the beans are tender turn up heat to medium high for 10 minutes or more to thicken liquid.

Serve over rice or with corn bread.

White Beans

Add 1 medium fresh tomato diced and 1—2 stalks celery diced to pot. Cook as directed for basic beans. You can add smoked polish sausage to the dish as well.

Black Beans

Add 1 diced tomato and jalapeño pepper to pot. Cook as directed for basic beans.

Black Eyed Peas

Use the same method for regular recipe and add 1 small diced tomato. Cooking time 1 1/2 hours.

Beans with Brick Chili

Add 1/2 pkg. of brick chili to the pinto bean recipe for a chili flavor.

Recipe for Joy

See the positive not the negative each day...

Surround yourself with happiness and peace...

Count your blessings not your sorrows...

Build strong faith and determination...

"Honesty is the first chapter in the book of wisdom."
Thomas Jefferson

Beans

Lentils

3 cups dried lentils

5—6 cups water

1 large onion diced

1/2 cup diced carrots

2 tsp. garlic powder or granules

2 tsp. seasoning salt

1 1/2 tsp. pepper

1/2—3/4 lb. bacon ends or ham chunks

Temperature: Stove top for 1 hour

Directions:

Mix all ingredients into a large pot. Heat over high heat until it comes to a boil. Lower heat to simmer and cover. Cook 45 minutes to an hour until beans are soft and the liquid has thickened. Add more water if needed. If it is too thin cook on high and let boil for 10 minutes to thicken. Lentils should be soft and thick not saucy. Serve over rice or wrap in lettuce leaves with the beans and rice.

Mongo (Mung) Beans

Use dry mung beans instead of lentils, add 1 additional cup of water, and add 1 cup fresh spinach leaves to pot (Filipino version). Cook as directed in lentil recipe.

Baked Beans

5 15oz. cans baked beans or pork and beans

1/4 cup ketchup

1/3 cup dark molasses

1—1 1/2 cups brown sugar

3 TBS. BBQ sauce

1 tsp. pepper

1 tsp. garlic powder or granules

1 tsp. onion powder

Temperature: Oven at 375 or 400 degrees for 45 minutes   Serves 6

Directions:

Put beans in a deep baking pan. Add all the ingredients and stir. Bake without a cover. Make sure you stir the mixture every 15 minutes. Stir more often during the last 15 minutes of cooking time. Beans are done when the liquid has thickened.

"Success is measured not so much by the position that one has reached in life as by the obstacles which one has overcome while trying to succeed."

Booker T. Washington

"We are shaped by our thoughts; we become what we think. When the mind is pure, joy follows like a shadow that never leaves." Buddha

Asian Dishes

Tempura

Egg Foo Yong

Lumpia

Pad Thai

Asian Dishes

Lumpia 1

1 1/2 lb. ground beef

1 TBS. olive oil or canola oil

3/4 cup diced onion

3/4 cup finely chopped celery

1 cup finely chopped cabbage

6 medium russet potatoes diced

4 cloves garlic minced

1 TBS. seasoning salt

2 tsp. garlic granules

1 1/2 tsp. pepper

1 pkg. spring roll wrappers

Temperature: Stove top for 20 minutes
Makes 16—20 rolls

Directions:

Brown meat with seasonings and drain. Sauté celery, cabbage, garlic, and onions in oil over medium high heat until soft then drain. Boil potatoes until soft then drain. Combine all ingredients together. Add more seasonings if needed. Let cool.

Fill spring roll wrapper with 2—3 large TBS. of filling. Roll tightly. Fry in hot oil until golden brown. Drain well. Serve with chinese chili sauce, sweet and sour sauce, or ketchup.

Variations:

Use ground turkey or diced shrimps instead of beef.

Add 1/2 cup raisins to meat.

Lumpia 2

Use ingredients for Lumpia 1

Use ground turkey instead of beef

Omit cabbage and celery

Use Chinese egg roll wrappers instead of spring roll wrappers

1/2 cup shredded carrots

12 oz. bean sprouts

8 oz. diced mushrooms

Directions:

In a pan on low heat cook potatoes, garlic, half of the seasonings, and onions with 2 TBS. oil. Cook until soft and lightly browned. (See Home Fried Potatoes in Sides section). Add more seasonings if needed. In another pan brown your meat, vegetables, and seasonings. Cook for 6—8 minutes. Drain well. Add more seasonings if needed. Mix the meat and potatoes together and roll into wrappers.

How To Fold Rolls

Method 1

Lay shell down like a rectangle. Put filling at one end, fold in both sides, then roll closed.

Method 2:

Place shell with pointed side up (diamond shape). Put filling on lower half of shell, fold sides in, then fold roll. You can buy Sweet Chili and spring roll wrappers at Filipino markets. Buy the thicker egg roll wrappers at your grocery.

Asian Dishes

Egg Foo Yong

12 oz. pkg. fresh bean sprouts

1/8 cup oil

1 TBS flour

4 eggs beaten

2 sliced green onions

1/2 tsp. garlic powder or granules

1/2 tsp. onion powder

Optional:

Diced cooked shrimps or cooked diced seasoned chicken (use the soy, ginger, garlic marinade on the chicken before cooking on page 89)

Temperature: Stove top for 15 minutes
Serves 3—4

Directions:

Add bean sprouts, seasonings, flour, eggs, onions, and meat (optional) and mix thoroughly in a bowl. Take a skillet and add a small amount of oil in it over medium heat. When skillet is hot add enough mixture to make a "pancake" size patty. Make sure you put some of the egg on it from the bottom of the bowl. Cover and cook for about 3 1/2 – 4 minutes and turn it over. It should be golden brown. Cover and cook the other side.

When all the patties are done use some watered down oyster sauce. Or make a sauce with 1 cup water, 1 TBS. corn starch, and 1—2 TBS. soy sauce. Cook sauce over low heat into a gravy consistency. Pour sauce over patties and enjoy.

Tempura

2 TBS. corn starch

1—2 TBS. ice water

1/4 tsp. salt

1 tsp. baking powder

3—4 egg whites

16 raw shrimps—deveined and fan cut

2 zucchinis & carrots—sliced like shoestring potatoes

8 small fresh mushrooms

Prep time 15 minutes   Serves 4

Directions:

Beat egg whites in a chilled bowl until stiff. Mix the flour, salt, and baking powder in a small bowl. Add the ice water and stir well. The mixture should be the consistency of pancake batter. Very gently fold mixture into the egg whites. Dip your shrimp and vegetables into the mixture and fry until golden brown.

Hint:

The trick to making this batter is to use chilled bowls, chilled beaters, and ice cold water.

"Go confidently in the direction of your dreams.
Live the life you have imagined." Henry David Thoreau

Asian Dishes

Basic Chow Mein

1 pkg. fresh chow mein or chinese noodles (you can find these in the produce area in the grocery store)

1/2 cup chopped cabbage

1/4 cup shredded carrots

1/3 cup chopped onions

Soy Sauce

1—1 1/2 TBS. oil

2 chopped green onions

Optional: Fresh bean sprouts

Temperature: Stove top in large skillet for 15 minutes   Serves 4

Directions:

Put oil in skillet over high heat. When hot add the cabbage, onions, and celery and stir fry for a few minutes. Add noodles to the pan and continue to stir fry until they are hot. Add soy sauce to taste as you continue frying the noodles. Add green onions at the end of the cooking time. If you want to add bean sprouts add them when the noodles start getting hot.

HINT:

You can use top ramen noodles for the chow mein noodles. Make sure you only cook them to separate them—they will be slightly cooked. Drain under cold water then add to the recipe.

Chicken Chow Mein

1—2 boneless chicken breasts

1/2 tsp. garlic powder or granules

1/2 tsp. ground ginger

1/4 cup soy sauce

1 1/2 TBS. oil

Basic chow mein recipe

Directions:

Marinate the chicken for at least 30 minutes in the in soy sauce and spices. Stir fry in very hot oil for 4 minutes. Follow the basic chow mien recipe to complete the dish.

Variations:

Use 1 lb. thinly sliced pork or beef instead of chicken. Make sure to marinate as directed.

Use 1 lb. raw shelled and deveined shrimps. Do not marinate. You can use frozen defrosted raw shrimps instead of fresh ones if you desire.

> *"Love many things, for therein lies the true strength, and whoso-ever loves much performs much, and can accomplish much, and what is done in love is done well."*
> Vincent van Gogh

*"Knowledge is proud that he has learn'd so much;
Wisdom is humble that he knows no more."* William Cowper

Asian Dishes

Basic Stir Fry

1—2 boneless chicken breasts

1/2 tsp. garlic powder or granules

1/2 tsp. ground ginger

1/4 cup soy sauce

Canola or vegetable oil

Vegetables—sliced on a diagonal

2—3 TBS. oyster sauce

Temperature: Stove top for 20 minutes
Serves 4—6

Directions:

Cut chicken breast in half the long way so the piece will be about 2 inches across. Slice the chicken into very thin slices—partially frozen meat will be easier to slice very thin. Put meat in a bowl with the spices and soy sauce. Marinate for 30 minutes. Cut your vegetables in 1/2 inch slices on the diagonal. Keep each vegetable type you cut separated; do not mix them together—they take different times to cook. Use onions, celery, bell peppers, zucchini, cabbage, bok choy, broccoli, mushrooms, or bean sprouts.

Make your skillet or wok as hot as you can on very high heat with 1—1 1/2 TBS oil in it. Add one kind of vegetable at a time. Do not mix the vegetables. Stir constantly flipping the vegetables according to the times listed below.

Remove cooked vegetable from pan and place in a container. Add more oil and let it get very hot again. Add next vegetable and stir fry. Remove and put in your container. When the vegetables are cooked make the pan very hot and add your meat with the marinade. Fry stirring constantly for about five or six minutes. Add the cooked vegetables to the pan and add the oyster sauce. Stir until well coated and mixed.

Cooking Times:

Start with the vegetables that take longest to cook first.

4—5 min.—Broccoli

3—3 1/2 min.—Bell pepper or zucchini

3 min.—Celery, onions, the white stock from bok choy

1—2 min.—Bean sprouts, mushrooms, chinese cabbage, tops of bok choy

Green onions—add at the end.

If you use this technique of cooking you will have a perfect stir fry every time. You can use beef, pork or shrimps for your meat or fried tofu.

You can stir fry noodles in oil and add before adding sauce.

Asian Dishes

Chicken Teriyaki

1 lb. chicken breasts

2 tsp. olive or canola oil

1 1/2 tsp. garlic powder

1 tsp. onion powder

1 tsp. pepper

1 pkg. teriyaki sauce mix or bottled sauce

Temperature: Stove top for 45 minutes
Serves 4

Directions:

Cut chicken breasts into 4 pieces or use chicken tenders. Brown on all sides in a large skillet. Season with garlic, onion, and pepper. Add water and simmer for twenty minutes. Add teriyaki sauce and continue to cook until chicken is tender.

Variation:

Add vegetables (cabbage, carrots, onions) to dish. Cut 1/2 cabbage into 4 wedges and cut out core. Cut one onion into wedges and add 3/4 cup baby carrots. Add to chicken dish half way through cooking (you can add it when you put in the sauce after 20 minutes).

Pancit Bihon

2 pkgs. dried rice sticks

1/2 cup chopped cabbage

1/2 cup shredded carrots

1/2 cup chopped onions

1 1/2 lbs. marinated chicken (thinly sliced- see page 89) or 1 lb. peeled shrimp

2 large tomatoes

6—8 cloves minced garlic

1/4 cup soy sauce

Temperature: Stove in large pot for 45 minutes Serves 6

Directions:

Soak noodles in cold water for 15—30 minutes. Drain well. Marinate chicken and let sit. Put oil in the skillet over high heat. When the pan is hot add the garlic and all the vegetables. Add the chicken or shrimp. Stir constantly until the vegetables start to soften and meat is cooked. Add drained noodles and stir constantly making sure you fold the mixture and heat all the noodles thoroughly.

When the noodles start to break apart add the soy sauce. Keep stirring until the rice noodles are in small pieces. Dish is done when the noodles are in 1/2 inch pieces.

Asian Dishes

Adobo (Filipino Meat)

1 1/2—2 lbs. chicken breasts or thighs or cubed pork

12 cloves of garlic (peeled)

1 TBS. peppercorns

1—1 1/2 cups white vinegar

Water

3 TBS. oil

2 TBS. butter or margarine

Salt and pepper to taste

Temperature: Stove top for 35—45 minutes   Serves 4

Directions:

Marinate chicken in white vinegar, garlic, and peppercorns for at least three hours or refrigerate overnight. Use a stainless steel, plastic, or glass container or a zip-lock bag to marinate. Remove chicken from vinegar and fry chicken with oil in skillet to brown it. Use the garlic cloves from the marinade with the chicken as it browns.

Add 1/2 cup of water and 1/2 cup of marinade liquid to pan and cover. Chicken should have at least an inch of liquid in the pan. Let simmer until chicken is tender. Do not let the liquid dry out while simmering. When tender remove chicken from pan. Put butter or margarine in pan juices and cook on medium high heat to make a sauce.

Add a little water if needed. Put the chicken back into pan and let the sauce coat the chicken. Add salt and pepper.

Pad Thai

4—5 pieces garlic chopped

1 small stick tofu—cut in bite size pieces (optional)

2 chopped green onions or chives

3/4 cup fresh bean sprouts

5 oz. thinly sliced chicken

8 oz. dry thai rice noodles—soaked and drained

1 egg

2 TBS. cooking oil

1 tsp. sugar

2 tsp. fish sauce

1 cup chicken stock

Temperature: Stove top for 20 minutes Serves 3

Directions:

Fry garlic in hot oil over low heat until light brown. Add chicken or tofu. Cook 1 min. Add egg, sugar, fish sauce, oyster sauce and mix together on high heat. Add noodles and immediately add water or chicken stock. Cook five minutes. Add sprouts and chives—cook 1 minute Serve with roasted crushed peanuts, chili powder, and lime.

"Don't grieve. Anything you lose comes round in another form."

Rumi

Side Dishes

Baked Mac and Cheese

Candied Yams

Whipped Yams

Potato Patties

Side Dishes

Stuffing

2 boxes Mrs. Cubisons Stuffing Mix (1 box corn bread, 1 box seasoned bread)

1 1/2 cubes melted margarine or butter

1 1/2—2 cups of water

2 cups coarsely chopped celery

1 cup coarsely chopped onion

1/2 bell pepper coarsely chopped

2 TBS chicken bouillon

1 tsp. garlic powder or granules

1 tsp. pepper

1 tsp. celery salt

1 TBS. seasoning salt

Temperature: Cooked in whole bird according to poultry recipe

Directions:

Coarsely chop onions, bell pepper, and celery. Put into a food processor with a small amount of water and chop until finely chopped.

Take 3 bags of stiffing mix (2 Corn Bread and 1 Bread) for a 10—12 lb. bird or 4 bags of stuffing mix for a 13—17 lb. bird and place in a very large mixing bowl or pan. Add the seasonings and vegetable mixture. Pour half of the water in and mix. Add more water until the mixture is very moist and holds together if you squeeze it with your fingers.

Stuff the cavity of your bird. Make sure you stuff it very tightly pushing it in to get as much inside as possible. If you have extra stuffing stuff it into the neck portion of the bird.

Make sure you pull the skin over the stuffed cavities to keep the stuffing moist during cooking. You can put a piece of foil over the stuffing if the skin does not completely cover the stuffed areas. Secure with a turkey trussing kit (metal picks and string).

Variations:

You can add other ingredients that you may like such as: mushrooms, green apple pieces, dried cranberries, or ground pork sausage.

If you prefer stuffing with big vegetable pieces coarsely chop your vegetables and do not blend them in the food processor.

"There is only one happiness in life, to love and be loved."
George Sand

Side Dishes

Fried Rice

2 cups cooked long grain rice

1 TBS. oil

2 cups water

Pinch of salt

1 beaten egg

Soy sauce

Chopped green onion

Temperature: Stove in pan for 15 minutes   Serves 4

Directions:

Use cold cooked day old rice for this recipe. Put oil in a large skillet on high heat. When oil is hot add cold rice. Make sure you break it apart with your hands before adding it so it won't be in big clumps. Fry the rice in oil until it is hot turning frequently. Add soy sauce to taste. Spread the rice apart in the middle to make a large hole in the rice. Put the egg in the exposed area of the pan. Scramble the egg until it is firm trying not the get it mixed into the rice. When it is cooked mix the egg with the rice. Sprinkle green onions into the rice. Add more soy sauce if needed.

Variation:

Add cooked chopped chicken, pork, or shrimp before you add the rice.

Spanish Rice

1 cup long grain rice

1 TBS. oil

1 7/8 cup water

1/4 cup tomato sauce or 1/3 cup crushed tomatoes

1/4 cup diced bell peppers

1/3 cup diced onion

1 1/2 TBS. chicken bouillon

1 tsp. taco seasoning mix

1/2 tsp. garlic powder or granules

1/2 tsp. pepper

Temperature: Stove top in small pot for 30 minutes   Serves 4

Directions:

Sauté rice over medium heat in oil until the rice turns white. Do not burn the rice. Add the rest of the ingredients and bring to a boil over high heat. Turn heat to low and cover and simmer until rice is fluffy and cooked.

"He who speaks without modesty ...
Will find it difficult to make his words good."
Confucius

Side Dishes

Easy Refried Beans

1 large can (29 oz.) pinto beans

1 tsp. garlic powder or granules

1 tsp. onion powder

1 tsp. taco seasoning

1 TBS. oil

Temperature: Stove top for 15 minutes
Serves 4

Directions:

Empty can of beans using only half of the liquid and seasonings into a skillet with hot oil. Use high heat. Mash beans with a potato masher. Keep mashing until beans are broken down and thickened. Serve with shredded cheese.

Scalloped Potatoes

3 large russet potatoes peeled and sliced into 1/8" slices

1 cube butter or margarine

1 cup milk

1/4 cup flour

Salt and pepper to taste

Temperature: Oven 350 degrees for 60 minutes   Serves 5—6

Directions:

Peel and cut potatoes into slices. Butter a baking pan or dish (square or rectangular ones work best). Place a layer of potato slices to cover the pan. Sprinkle with seasonings. Sprinkle with flour. Dot with butter or margarine. Keep layering as directed until the pan is full or you run out of potatoes. Pour milk into pan until it almost reaches the top of the last layer. Bake until golden brown, tender, and the liquid is thick. You can add shredded cheese to the layers and on top if desired.

Fried Green Tomatoes

2 green tomatoes sliced

1 beaten egg with 1TBS. water

Seasoned bread crumbs

Canola oil for frying

Temperature: Fry in skillet for 15 minutes Serves 4

Directions:

Take tomato slices and dip in egg mixture. Completely coat the slices with bread crumbs. Fry in hot oil until golden brown and tender. Drain on paper towel.

Side Dishes

Potato Patties

2 cups leftover mashed potatoes

1 egg

3/4 cup flour

Oil for frying

Temperature: Fry in skillet for 15 minutes   Serves 4

Directions:

Take mashed potatoes and add egg. Mix well. Form into thick patties. Roll patties in flour making sure that they are well coated and completely covered. Fry in hot oil until golden brown and crispy. Drain well. This makes a good morning breakfast potato patty or you can use it as a dinner side dish.

Variations:

Add shredded cheese into the potato mixture before forming patties.

Season potato mixture with garlic and onion powder.

Add diced onions, cheddar cheese, and crumbled bacon to mixture before forming patties.

Home Fried Potatoes

2 large potatoes diced or sliced

1 onion diced or sliced

1/2 tsp. garlic powder or granules

1/2 tsp. pepper

1/4—1/2 tsp. seasoning salt

1/8 cup oil

Temperature: Fry in skillet for 20—30 minutes   Serves 3—4

Directions:

Put oil in bottom of skillet and heat over medium heat. Add potatoes and all other ingredients. Cook on medium low heat covered until potatoes are soft. Remove cover and turn heat up to medium high. When bottom side of potatoes are golden brown turn them over and brown other side.

Variation:

If you like a crispy potato do not cover the pan. Fry the potatoes until golden brown on each side. Add bell peppers if desired.

Side Dishes

Twice Baked Potatoes

2—3 large potatoes baked

2 TBS. butter or margarine

2—3 TBS. milk

Salt and pepper to taste

1/4 cup melted butter or margarine

1/3 cup seasoned bread crumbs

Temperature: Oven 400 degrees for 15 minutes   Serves 4—6

Directions:

Bake potatoes. Cut in half lengthwise. Scoop out the cooked potatoes and put into a bowl. Leave about 1/2 inch of potatoes on the skin. Save the skins and do not break them when you scoop them out. Mash potatoes with a potato masher while they are still hot. Add the unmelted margarine and stir with a fork. Add milk and seasonings. Continue whipping the potatoes with your fork until they are a fluffy consistency. Put the mashed potato mixture back into the skins. Drizzle the melted butter on top of the potato and sprinkle with the bread crumbs. Bake until top is golden and crusty.

Variations:

Add shredded cheese before baking.

Add garlic to mashed potatoes.

Fried Cabbage

1 whole cabbage chopped

4 slices of bacon cut in pieces

3/4 cup diced onion

1/3 cup water

1 tsp. garlic powder or granules

1 tsp. pepper

1 tsp. seasoning salt

Temperature: Stove top in pot for 20 minutes   Serves 5—6

Directions:

Sauté bacon in pot until cooked but not crispy. Add cabbage and onions. Cook over medium heat. Stir constantly until the cabbage starts getting soft. Add water and simmer covered until cabbage is soft and well flavored.

Variations:

Add sliced or diced carrots.

Add two large potatoes diced.

"I have discovered the secret that after climbing a great hill, one only finds that there are many more hills to climb." Nelson Mandela

Side Dishes

Sautéed Zucchini

3 large zucchini sliced 1/8" thick

1 large diced tomato

1 cup diced onions

Salt & pepper to taste

2 tsp. seasoning salt

1 1/2 tsp. garlic granules

2 TBS. olive or canola oil

1/2 cup shredded cheese

Temperature: Stove top in large skillet for 25 minutes   Serves 4

Directions:

Sauté zucchini, chopped tomatoes, and chopped onions in olive oil over medium high heat until squash starts getting soft stirring often. Add the seasonings. Cover and simmer about 20 minutes until done. Zucchini will be soft and translucent. Add cheese across the top. Cook 1—2 minutes with lid on to melt cheese.

Variation:

Use diced eggplant, sliced okra, or yellowsquash instead of zucchini. Or use 2 cups broccoli and no tomatoes.

Green Beans

1 1/2—2 lbs. string beans

4 slices of bacon cut in pieces

3/4 cup diced onion

Water to cover beans

1 1/2 tsp. garlic powder

1 tsp. pepper

2 tsp. seasoning salt

Temperature: Stove top in pot for 45 minutes   Serves 4—6

Directions:

Sauté bacon in pot until cooked but not crispy over medium high heat. Add string beans that have been cleaned, stringed, and broken into pieces. Stir constantly until the beans start to get a little soft (about 10 minutes). Cover beans with water and add onions and seasonings. Simmer covered until beans are soft and well flavored.

"Action may not always bring happiness ... but there is no happiness without action." *Benjamin Disraeli*

Side Dishes

Greens

3 bunches collard greens

2—3 bunches texas mustard greens

3/4 lb. bacon ends, or ham chunks, or 2 ham hocks, or smoked turkey thigh or leg

1 large diced onion

1/3 cup water

1 tsp. garlic powder or granules

2 tsp. pepper

2 tsp. seasoning salt

1 TBS beef bouillon

1 TBS. sugar

1 TBS. oil

Water to cover greens when they have wilted

Temperature: Stove top in large pot for 2—2 1/2 hours   Serves 6

Directions:

Wash and clean greens. Make sure that you remove the entire stem all the way into the leaf area. Make sure you wash well. Tear or cut the greens into small pieces. Add oil to large pot and add greens over medium high heat. Fill the pot 3/4 full. Keep turning the greens to keep them from burning and help them to wilt. Add more raw greens and keep stirring as the greens wilt and there is more space in the pot for all the greens.

When the greens are wilted add the rest of the ingredients. Cover the mixture with water making sure that the water level is slightly above the top of the greens. Bring to a boil and reduce heat to low. Simmer covered until greens are tender and flavorful. If you have to add more seasonings do so. Make sure you check the greens periodically and add more water if needed.

Variation:

Use all collard greens if desired.

Add three medium peeled and diced turnips to the recipe. Add when you add all the ingredients to the pot.

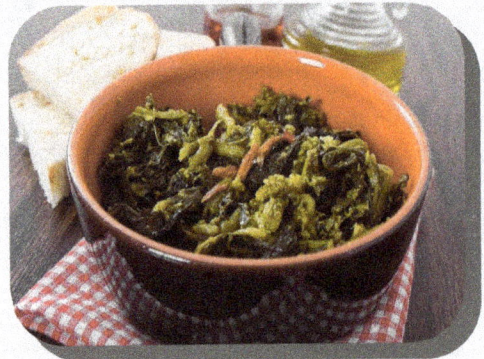

"It does not matter how slowly you go as long as you do not stop." Confucius

"The greatest test of courage on earth is to bear defeat without losing heart." Robert G. Ingersoll

Side Dishes

Stuffed Zucchini

2 large zucchinis

1 cup diced onion

1 large tomato diced

1/2 cup diced mushrooms

1/3 tsp. italian seasoning

1 tsp. pepper

1 tsp. salt

2 tsp. garlic powder or chopped garlic

1 cup shredded cheddar cheese

1/2 cup seasoned bread crumbs

Temperature: Oven 350 degrees for 35—45 minutes or until tender
Serves 4

Directions:

Scrape the seeds and seed center from the squash cut lengthwise. Scrape out 1/2 of the flesh and chop finely. Mix squash, vegetables, and seasonings. Put into the squash shell. Sprinkle with breadcrumbs and cheese. Bake in a shallow baking pan until squash is tender. Add extra breadcrumbs and cheese during the last five minutes of cooking.

Variation:

Stuff with meatloaf mix or ground meat mix (ground beef, seasoning, and fresh breadcrumbs), or uncooked seasoned ground beef mixed with rice and mushrooms. Cover stuffed squash boat with tomato sauce and parmesan cheese. Bake as in recipe above.

Candied Yams

8 small yams

1/2 can diced pineapple

2—3 cups dark brown sugar

1/2 cup butter or margarine cut in pieces

3/4 tsp. cinnamon

2 tsp. vanilla extract

1/4 tsp. ground cloves

1/4 tsp. ground nutmeg

Temperature: Oven 350 degrees for 40—50 minutes   Serves 6

Directions:

Peel and cut yams into slices 3/4 inch thick. Make the pieces the same size to help them cook at the same time. Place yams and pineapple in a deep baking pan. Mix the spices and sprinkle over the yams. Add 1/8 cup of the pineapple syrup from the pineapple. Sprinkle brown sugar and margarine over the yams. Bake until tender and glazed. Baste yams often during the cooking process to help them glaze evenly.

Side Dishes

Whipped Yams

2 large cans whole yams or 4—5 large yams boiled and peeled

1 TBS. vanilla extract

1 1/2 tsp. cinnamon

3/4 tsp. allspice

1/2 tsp. nutmeg

2 cups sugar

2 large eggs

1 cube butter or margarine melted

2 oz. defrosted concentrated orange juice

Temperature: Oven 350 degrees for 45—60 minutes   Serves 6

Directions:

Grease baking dish with margarine. Put yams in a mixing bowl and use mixer to mash the yams. Whip the potatoes to remove excess lumps and strings. Add the dry ingredients and mix to combine them. Add the melted margarine and mix. Beat the eggs in a separate bowl until they turn light yellow and fluffy. Carefully fold the eggs into the potato mixture a little at a time. Add orange juice and mix on low until well blended. Pour into pan and bake until done.

Potato Salad

8—10 whole medium potatoes

1 medium onion coarsely chopped

3/4 bell pepper coarsely chopped

4 stalks of celery coarsely chopped

3 hard boiled eggs diced

2—3 tsp. mustard

3—4 TBS sweet relish

3/4—1 cup mayonnaise

1 tsp. pepper

1 tsp. garlic powder or granules

2—3 tsp. seasoning salt

Prep time 45 minutes   Serves 5—6

Directions:

Boil whole potatoes in pot with water covering them and cook until tender. Let potatoes cool. Take coarsely chopped onions, celery, and bell pepper and put in a food processor. Chop until fine. Peel and dice potatoes. If the potatoes are still hot dice them in big pieces. If they are completely cold then cut them a bit smaller.

Hint: The hot potatoes will get smaller when you are mixing the dish. I usually make it with hot potatoes.

Add mayonnaise and spices. Mix well. If the salad is too dry add a little more mayo. Add more seasonings if needed.

Side Dishes

Stove Top Mac and Cheese

3 TBS. flour

1/4 cup margarine or butter

1 tsp. chicken bouillon

3 cups shredded cheddar cheese

Salt and pepper to taste

2 cups milk

1 8 oz. pkg. elbow macaroni

Temperature: Stove top for 25 minutes
Serves 4—6

Directions:

Cook pasta until done. Melt margarine in a saucepan over medium heat. Gradually add flour while stirring with a wire whisk. Do not brown the flour and do not let it get lumpy. When the flour is mixed in gradually add milk stirring with the whisk constantly. Let simmer for 5—10 minutes until the flour taste is gone. Add the chicken seasoning and salt and pepper. Taste to make sure it is seasoned well.

Gradually add the shredded cheese to the sauce stirring as you add it. When all the cheese is melted add your pasta. Mix well. Add more pepper if needed. This recipe makes a creamy and cheesy stove top mac and cheese dish.

Baked Mac & Cheese Recipe One

4 TBS. flour

4 TBS. margarine or butter

1 tsp. chicken bouillon

2 cups shredded cheddar cheese

1 cup shredded colby cheese

Salt and pepper to taste

2 cups milk

12 oz. elbow macaroni

1/2 cup cheese for top of dish

Temperature: Stove top for 30—35 minutes   Serves 4—6

Directions:

Cook as directed in stove top recipe but only add colby cheese to the sauce. Add the sauce to cooled noodles then add the cheese to the noodle mixture. Pour into a greased baking dish. Sprinkle cheese across the top and bake to golden brown.

"Honesty is the first chapter in the book of wisdom." *Thomas Jefferson*

Side Dishes

Baked Mac and Cheese Recipe Two

12—16 oz. elbow macaroni

1 8 oz. jar of Cheese Wiz

8—12 oz. of shredded sharp cheddar cheese

8—12 oz. of shredded mild cheddar cheese

3 cups milk

2 large eggs

2 tsp. chicken bouillon

Salt and pepper to taste

1 stick butter or margarine

Temperature: Bake at 350 degrees for 45 minutes   Serves 6

Directions:

Cook pasta until done. Drain and cool. Grease a baking dish with margarine. Put cooked pasta into dish and add the cube of margarine or butter cut into pieces and spread throughout the dish. Stir in Cheese Wiz. In a bowl add the eggs and milk. Beat until well blended and the eggs are well mixed. Add seasonings and mix again. Add all the egg mixture to the pasta and the cheeses and mix well. Sprinkle cheese across the top. Bake until dish is lightly brown and hot throughout.

Greek Vegetables

3 large potatoes cut in strips

4—5 carrots cut in strips

1 large zucchini cut in strips

1 onion cut in half and sliced

1/4 cup olive oil

4 cloves minced garlic

1 tsp. salt

1 1/2 tsp. pepper

1 TBS. beef bouillon

Temperature: Bake at 375 degrees for 30—40 minutes   Serves 4

Directions:

Cut zucchini, potatoes, and carrots in slices like you would for french fries. Sprinkle with the spices. Toss the vegetables and onions with the olive oil. Bake on a foil lined pan covered with foil for 20 minutes. Stir and cook uncovered until the vegetables are tender and browned.

> *"When you are content to be simply yourself and don't compare or compete... Everybody will respect you."*
>
> *Lau Tzu*

"The person attempting to travel two roads at once will get nowhere."
Xun Zi

Salads

Waldorf
Spring Salad

Italian Pasta Salad

Cole Slaw

Pasta Salad

Salads

Seafood Salad

1 medium onion diced

1/2 cup bell pepper diced

3/4 cups celery diced

2 cups cooked shrimp or imitation crab chunks, cut into small pieces

1/3—1/2 cup mayonnaise

1 tsp. pepper

1/2 tsp. garlic powder or granules

2 tsp. seasoning salt

1/2 tsp. lemon juice

1/4 tsp. red pepper flakes

1/4 tsp. dried parsley or 1/2 TBS. fresh chopped parsley

Prep time 20 minutes   Serves 4—6

Directions:

Dice onions, celery, and bell pepper and put in a mixing bowl. Add spices and mayonnaise. Mix well. If the salad is too dry add a little more mayo. Add more seasonings if needed. Refrigerate and serve cold.

Cucumber Salad

1—2 large cucumbers peeled and thinly sliced

1 large onion thinly sliced

1/4—1/3 cup white vinegar

2 TBS. olive oil

1 tsp. pepper

Salt to taste

1/2 tsp. garlic powder

1/2—1 TBS. sugar

Prep time 15 minutes   Serves 4

Directions:

Slice onions and cucumbers into thin slices and put in a mixing bowl. Add the oil, vinegar, and spices. Mix well. If the salad is too tart add a little more sugar. If the vinegar is too strong add a little more oil. Refrigerate until ready to eat.

Fruit Salad

1 cantaloupe

1/2 small—medium watermelon

1 pint fresh strawberries

3/4 cup fresh blueberries

1—2 cups fresh blackberries

1 8 oz. can mandarin oranges

2 cups fresh pineapple pieces or 1 can chunk pineapple

Prep time 20 minutes   Serves 6—8

Directions:

Make melon balls with the cantaloupe and watermelon. You can use a melon ball spoon or a small measuring spoon to make the balls. Mix all the fruits together with 1/3 cup sugar. Serve chilled in hollowed out watermelon rind.

"Everything has its beauty but not everyone sees it."
Confucius

Salads

Pasta Salad

1 medium onion diced

1/2 cup bell pepper diced

3/4 cups celery diced

3/4—1 cup mayonnaise

1 tsp. pepper

1/2 tsp. garlic powder or granules

2 tsp. seasoning salt

1/4 tsp. dried parsley or 1/2 TBS. chopped fresh parsley

8 oz. pasta

Prep time 25 minutes   Serves 6

Directions:

Cook pasta (elbow, small shells, rotini, or penne) to make 3—4 cups cooked pasta. Dice onions, celery, and bell pepper and put in a mixing bowl. Add cooled pasta. Add mayonnaise and spices. Mix well. If the salad is too dry add a little more mayo. Add more seasonings if needed. Refrigerate and serve cold.

Variation:

Add 3 diced hard boiled eggs.

Use vegetable flavored spiral pasta.

Ham Salad

1 1/2 cups diced cooked ham

3/4 cooked frozen peas (optional)

Add ingredients to basic pasta salad recipe. Mix well and chill.

Chicken Salad

1 1/2 cups diced cooked chicken

2 hard boiled eggs diced (optional)

Add ingredients to basic pasta salad recipe. Mix well and chill. Garnish with hard boiled eggs.

Shrimp Salad

2 cups cooked shrimp

1/8 tsp. cayenne pepper

1 tsp. fresh lemon juice

Add ingredients to basic pasta salad recipe. Chill and serve.

Wise men talk because they have something to say; fools, because they have to say something." Plato

Salads

Italian Pasta Salad

8 oz. pasta (4 cups cooked)

1 medium onion diced

1/2 cup bell pepper diced

3/4 cups celery diced

1/2 cup italian dressing

1 12 oz. can drained kidney beans

3/4 cup lightly cooked sliced frozen carrots

1/2 cup lightly cooked frozen broccoli florets

1 tsp. pepper

1/2 tsp. garlic powder or granules

1 tsp. seasoning salt

1/4 tsp. dried parsley or 1/2 TBS. chopped fresh parsley

1/2 cup garbanzo beans (optional)

Prep time 25 minutes   Serves 4

Directions:

Cook pasta (elbow, rotini, or penne) to make 3—4 cups cooked pasta. Cook frozen vegetables until they are still very crispy. Cool under cold water to stop cooking process and drain. Put beans and vegetables in mixing bowl. Add cooled pasta, dressing, and spices. Mix well. If the salad is too dry add a little more italian dressing. Add more seasonings if needed. Refrigerate and serve cold.

Seafood Pasta Salad

1 1/2 cups diced shrimp or imitation crab

Ingredients for Italian Pasta Salad

Follow the Italian Pasta Salad recipe and add the seafood at the end. You can garnish it with hard boiled eggs cut in half lengthwise.

Three Bean Salad

1 medium onion sliced

1/2 cup italian dressing

1 15 oz. can drained kidney beans

1 15 oz. can drained cut string beans

1 15 oz. can drained garbanzo beans or any other canned bean you prefer

1 tsp. pepper

1/2 tsp. garlic powder or granules

1 tsp. seasoning salt

Prep time 15 minutes   Serves 4

Directions:

Slice onions and put in a mixing bowl. Add the beans. Add dressing and spices. Mix well. If the salad is too dry add a little more italian dressing. Add more seasonings if needed. Refrigerate. Optional: add 1 cup cooked pasta.

"Not engaging in ignorance is wisdom."
Bodhidharma

Salads

Coleslaw

1 medium cabbage cut into quarters and then thinly sliced

1 cup shredded carrots

3/4 cup mayonnaise

1/4—1/3 sweet pickle juice

1/4 tsp. mustard

1 TBS. sugar

1 tsp. pepper

1/2 tsp. garlic powder or granules

1/4 tsp. seasoning salt

1 tsp. milk (optional)

Prep time 20 minutes   Serves 4—6

Directions:

Cut cabbage into quarters or 6 wedges and remove the core. Thinly slice the wedges. Add the cabbage and carrots to a mixing bowl

Dressing:

Add mayonnaise, pickle juice, mustard, and seasonings and mix well. If the mixture is too sweet add more mayo. If it is too sour add more sugar. Pour over vegetables and mix well. Chill.

Waldorf Spring Salad

3—4 cups spring mix lettuce

1 1/2 cups fresh spinach

3 sliced radishes

1/2 cup cherry or grape tomatoes

1/3 cup shredded carrots

1/2 sliced small purple onion

1/4 cup cranraisins

1/4 cup glazed walnuts or pecans

1 small can mandarin oranges drained

Raspberry or Balsamic Vinegar dressing

Prep Time: 20 minutes   Serves 6

Directions:

Put lettuce and spinach in a bowl. Add in carrots and radishes and mix. Add your tomatoes, onions, and green-onions. Do not mix in. Sprinkle the mandarin oranges across the top. Then top off with the glazed nuts.

You can add sliced or slivered almonds across the top if desired. Serve with your favorite dressing or the dressings suggested.

For a complete meal add grilled or diced chicken to the salad.

Summer Fruit & Salad

Use the Waldorf Spring Salad recipe. Omit the radishes and add 3/4 cup fresh strawberries, 1/3 cup fresh blue-berries, and 1/3 cup diced pineapple. Add 1/3 cup slivered almonds to the salad.

"Our greatest glory is not in never falling, but in getting up every time we do."   *Confucius*

Breakfast

French Toast

Omelet

Breakfast Hash

Easy Donuts

Breakfast

Huevos Rancheros

4 fried eggs

1 15 oz. can refried beans

4 corn tortillas

1 cup salsa

3/4 cup shredded cheese

Temperature: Oven at 350 degrees for 20 minutes   Serves 4

Directions:

Warm corn tortillas in oil to make them pliable and drain on a paper towel. Put foil on a baking sheet. Spray with a cooking release spray or coat with a thin layer of oil. Place tortillas in pan in a single layer. Put the refried beans on top of the tortilla. Place a fried egg on top then put salsa on top of the egg. Top with shredded cheese. Bake until hot in oven.

Variation:

Put a layer of sour cream on top of the tortilla. Add chopped olives and green onions on top of the salsa.

Serve with guacamole.

Honie's Easy Donuts

1 can buttermilk biscuits

Oil for frying

Toppings

"No act of kindness, no matter how small, is ever wasted."   Aesop

Temperature: Stove in large skillet for 10—12 minutes   Serves 6

Directions:

Put oil in skillet over medium high heat. Take each biscuit and make a hole in the middle of it. The biscuit will look like a tire. Fry until golden brown and drain well.

Toppings:

Sprinkle with some cinnamon sugar, powdered sugar, drizzle with chocolate, lemon, or vanilla glaze.

Chocolate or vanilla glaze:

Melt 1/3 cup chocolate or vanilla frosting in a microwave for 10—12 seconds. Stir well and then drizzle over warm donuts. You may also use one of the glazes in the toppings section of this cookbook.

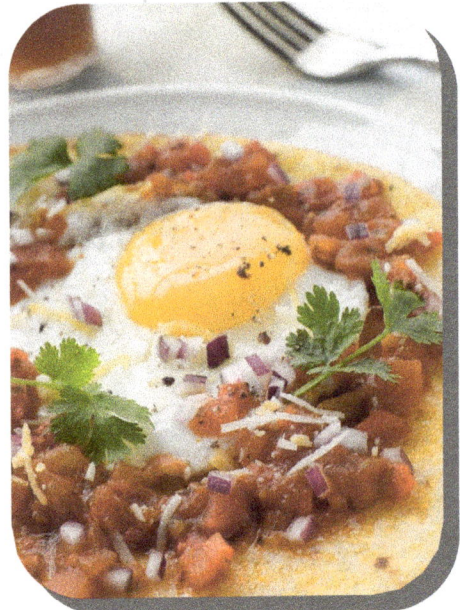

Breakfast

French Toast— Traditional

2—3 slices of bread cut into 4—6 triangle wedges

2 eggs beaten

1 tsp. vanilla extract

1 tsp. cinnamon

2 TBS. pancake mix

1/3—1/2 cup milk

3—4 TBS. canola oil

3—4 TBS. margarine or butter

Temperature: Stove top in large skillet for 15 minutes   Serves 2—3

Directions:

Cut each piece of bread cross ways to make 2 triangles. You can use thick sliced bread, regular bread, raisin bread, or any sliced bread except french bread. Take eggs, vanilla, cinnamon, pancake mix, and milk then mix well. Put pieces of bread into the mixture. Let them soak for 5—10 minutes before cooking.

Put equal parts margarine and oil in a thick skillet (I use the black cast iron skillet) until it is melted. Add french toast and cook over medium heat until it is golden brown then turn over and cook other side.

French Toast Pastry

2—3 slices of bread cut into 4—6 triangle wedges

1 tsp. vanilla extract

1 1/2 tsp. cinnamon

1 cup pancake mix

Water or milk to make a thick pancake batter (follow pancake mix directions)

Oil for frying

Temperature: Stove top in large skillet for 15 minutes

Directions:

Cut each piece of bread cross ways to make 2 triangles. You can use thick sliced bread, regular bread, raisin bread, or any sliced bread except french bread. You can fit about 3 pieces of toast in a pan at a time. Sprinkle cinnamon on bread slices. Take pancake batter and add vanilla and cinnamon. Make the batter a little thicker than you would for pancakes.

Fry in hot oil over medium heat until crispy and golden brown on both sides. This makes a french toast that is crunchy, thick, and more like a fried pastry. You can finish it off with sprinkled powdered sugar. Serve with whipped cream and Honies Strawberry Glaze for a sweet treat.

"I tore myself away from the safe comfort of certainties through my love for truth - and truth rewarded me. " Simone de Beauvoir

Breakfast

Basic Omelet

2 eggs beaten

1/3 cup shredded cheese

3—4 diced mushrooms

1/4 cup diced onion

Seasoning salt to taste

Pepper to taste

Temperature: Stove in large skillet for 10 minutes   Serves 1

Directions:

Sauté vegetables in olive oil. Grease your skillet well or spray with non-stick cooking spray. Pour eggs into skillet. Make sure the eggs cover the pan surface. Add cooked vegetables to one half of omelet. Sprinkle seasoning on vegetables. Add cheese. Cook on low heat covered for about 5 minutes. The egg should be set and not runny inside. Once it is set gently fold it in half putting the side with no vegetables on top. Cook for one minute then very carefully remove from pan.

Variations:

- Add crumbled cooked bacon or diced ham
- Add cooked fresh diced tomatoes
- Add cooked asparagus, spinach, or potatoes
- Use canned chili instead of veggies

Jazzed Up Pancakes

1 tsp. cinnamon

1 tsp. vanilla extract

Chopped nuts (optional)

Pancake mix

Add cinnamon and vanilla to your favorite pancake mix recipe. Your pancakes will have a nice spicy flavor. You can add chopped nuts to the batter for a little crunch.

Variation:

Add 1/2—3/4 cup mini chocolate chips or frozen blueberries to batter

Breakfast Potato Hash

1 recipe Home Fried Potatoes

1 cup sliced hot dogs or polish sausage, bacon or diced ham, cooked sausage or any cooked breakfast meat

1/3 cup diced bell pepper

Temperature: Stove top in large skillet for 15 minutes   Serves 4—5

Directions:

Add bell peppers to the home fried potatoes recipe (p. 69). Fry meat in a skillet to brown and cook it. Add meat to potatoes 5 minutes before potatoes are done cooking.

""If a man in the morning hears the right way, he may die in the evening without regret."   *Confucius*

Sauces & Batters

Fried Fish Batter

Folding Whipped Eggs

Brown Gravy

Honie's BBQ Sauce

Sauces & Batters

Brown Gravy

1/4 cup flour

1/2 tsp. onion powder

1 TBS. beef bouillon

Salt and pepper to taste

2 cups water

Oil or pan drippings

Prep time 15 minutes Serves 4—6

Directions:

Heat oil in skillet on medium high until hot. You can use roast pan drippings instead of oil. Add flour 1 TBS. at a time mixing with a metal spatula. Brown the flour until it is crumbly. For dark gravy make the flour golden brown. Gradually add water mixing constantly holding the spatula parallel to the pan. Use it to break up any lumps or use a wire wisk.

Once gravy is well mixed with no lumps add the seasoning and reduce heat to low. If you have pan drippings add about 3—4 TBS. of it. Let simmer until thick. The simmering will make the sauce lose the flour taste and become flavorful.

Turkey Gravy

Use the directions above. Substitute chicken bouillon or stock for the beef. Brown your flour to a medium brown for a light colored gravy. Use pan drippings from your roast if you have them.

White Sauce

1 TBS. margarine or butter

1/4 cup flour

1—1 1/2 cups water

1/2 tsp. chicken bouillon

Salt & pepper to taste

Prep time 15 minutes Serves 4—6

Directions:

Melt butter in saucepan. Add flour a little at a time to the butter. Stir it around being careful to get out any lumps. Do not brown the flour. Add water gradually and stir constantly. You can use a wire wisk if you like. Add pepper, 1/2 tsp. chicken bouillon, and salt to taste. Let simmer on low for 10 minutes to get rid of the flour taste. Make sure you add additional water or seasonings if needed.

Cheese Sauce

Use the while sauce recipe above. Add 1 cup shredded cheddar cheese to the cooked sauce and stir until melted.

Folding Whipped Eggs

Separate the egg yolks and whites. Beat the egg whites until stiff. Beat the egg yolks until light and fluffy. Gently pour the egg yolks into the egg whites and fold carefully.

Sauces & Batters

Honie's BBQ Sauce

1 bottle hickory or sweet BBQ sauce (buy a name brand)

1 tsp. pepper

1 tsp. garlic powder

1 tsp. bbq seasoning

1 tsp. monterey steak spice

1/2 tsp. cajun spice

1/2 cup brown sugar

1/4 tsp. liquid smoke (optional)

Prep time 10 minutes

Directions:

Put store made bbq sauce in a bowl and add the spices and brown sugar. Mix well. You can add more cajun spice if you like it hot or tabasco sauce. Save your jar and put any unused portion back into the jar for future use.

Fried Fish Batter

1 cup corn meal

1 cup corn starch

1 tsp. pepper

1 tsp. garlic powder or granules

1 tsp. onion powder

2 tsp. Chef Maritos fish seasoning or any spicy fish seasoning you like

1/2 tsp. paprika

Prep time 10 minutes

Directions:

Add all the ingredients and mix well. This makes a batter that is very light yet crispy and crunchy.

Asian Marinade

1 tsp. powdered ginger

1 tsp. garlic powder or granules

1/2 cup soy sauce

2 TBS. water

Use this to marinate your sliced beef, pork, and chicken in asian dishes. Marinate 30 minutes to overnight in your refrigerator. For a hot marinade add 3—4 drops tabasco sauce and 1 tsp. brown sugar.

Fish Marinade

1/2 cup olive oil

4 cloves minced garlic

1 tsp. dried minced onion

1 tsp. dried parsley

1/2 tsp. paprika

1 tsp. dried rosemary or cumin

1/8 cup lemon juice

Mix all ingredients. Let fish marinate for 30—45 minutes.

"Everyone has been made for some particular work, and the desire for that work has been put in every heart." Rumi

Desserts & More

Honie's Cheesecake

Cake Bon Bons

Fruit & Pudding Cups and
Fruit & Cake Cups

Oatmeal & Chocolate
Chip Cookies

Desserts & More

Berry Topping

1 can frozen sweetened strawberries or 1 bag frozen strawberries

1/4—2/3 cup sugar

1 TBS. cornstarch

1/3—2/3 cup water

Temperature: Stove top in saucepan for 15 minutes   Makes 1 1/2—2 cups

Directions:

Sweetened Berries:

Defrost frozen berries then add to a saucepan. Add 1/4 - 1/3 cup sugar to berries. Mix cornstarch in a cup with 1/3 cup water. Add to berry mixture and let cook on medium low heat until thick. Let cool.

Unsweetened Berries:

Place frozen berries in a saucepan with 1/2—2/3 cups of water and 2/3 cups of sugar. Add cornstarch mixed with 1/4 cup cold water. Bring to boil then cook over medium low heat until thick. Let cool.

Use as a topping on your cheesecake, tarts, or mix into fillings.

Variations:

Use frozen peaches, frozen mangos, or frozen mixed berries instead of strawberries.

Honie's Cake Filling

1 pkg. instant pudding

1 qt. Pastry Pride Whipped Topping (Smart & Final sells it)

Fruit topping or pudding cups

Prep time 12 minutes Fills a 9" cake

Directions:

Defrost whipped topping in carton. Chill your mixing bowl and electric beater blades well. Pour in 1/3 carton of the whipped topping. Whip on high until it forms soft peaks. Add pudding mix and beat until fluffy and stiff. Fold in fresh berries, berry topping, or pudding. Use as a filling for your favorite cakes.

For chocolate filling use chocolate pudding mix. For all others use vanilla. Defrosted topping (not whipped yet) may be refrozen for future use.

Cream Cheese Frosting

1 8 oz. pkg. softened cream cheese

1/2 cup softened butter or margarine

2 tsp. vanilla extract

6 cups powdered sugar sifted

Prep Time: 15 minutes Frosts a 2 layer 8" cake or 1 layer sheet cake

Directions:

Beat all the ingredients except the sugar with an electric mixer until fluffy. Gradually add sugar while beating. Frosting should be fluffy and easy to spread.

Desserts & More

Whip Cream Frosting

1 quart carton Pastry Pride Whipped Topping (buy at Smart & Final)

Prep time 10 minutes

Directions:

Defrost whipped topping in carton. Chill your mixing bowl and electric beater blades well. Pour in 1/2 carton of the whipped topping. Whip on high until it has a firm whipped cream texture and medium peaks.

Whip Cream Frosting for Cake Decorating

Follow recipe above. Whip until the topping forms stiff peaks. DO NOT overbeat because it will solidify. If you over beat it add a little liquid whipped topping and beat until it is stiff.

Banana Nut Bread

1/3 cup butter or margarine

1/2 cup sugar

2 eggs

1 3/4 cup sifted flour

1 tsp. baking powder

1/2 tsp. baking soda

1/2 tsp. salt

1 cup mashed ripe bananas

1/2 cup chopped walnuts

1/2 tsp. ground cinnamon

1 tsp. vanilla extract

1/2 cup raisins (optional)

Temperature: Bake for 350 for 40—45 minutes

Directions:

Put butter and sugar in bowl and beat with an electric mixer until light and fluffy. Add eggs to mixture one at a time and beat between each egg. Sift the flour and dry ingredients together. Add half the flour and half the bananas to the creamed butter and beat until blended. Add the rest of the flour and bananas and beat until well blended. Add in the vanilla and mix. Stir in the walnuts and raisins by hand.

Pour into a greased and floured (use my cake pan coating recipe if desired) 9.5x5x3 loaf pan and bake. When done remove from pan and cool on wire rack.

Variation:

- Add 3/4 cup chocolate chips instead of raisins to batter

- Add 1/2 cup cranraisins instead of regular raisins

- Dust with powdered sugar when done or lightly glaze with my vanilla glaze

"Don't waste yourself in rejection, nor bark against the bad, but chant the beauty of the good. "   Ralph Waldo Emerson

Desserts & More

Easy Glazes

1 cup powdered sugar

2 tsp. vanilla extract

1 TBS. milk

or

1 ready made frosting in tub

Prep time 10 minutes

Directions:

Mix the dry ingredients until smooth and creamy. If it is too thick add more milk or too thin add more powdered sugar. Use other flavor extracts for variation. If you use lemon juice use 1 1/2 tsp. lemon juice and 1 1/2 tsp. milk and omit vanilla.

Ready made frosting recipe:

Melt the ready made frosting in a microwave for 15 seconds. Mix with a spoon. If it is still too thick microwave a few seconds at a time. Use as a drizzle glaze on your cakes, donuts, or any other item you want to glaze.

Fudge Frosting

3 cups powdered sugar sifted

2/3 cup unsweetened cocoa powder

1 stick butter softened

1/3 cup milk

1 tsp. vanilla extract

Prep time 12 minutes

Directions:

Beat margarine and milk with an electric mixer until fluffy. Gradually add the cocoa and mix. Gradually add the sugar while beating. Add vanilla. Frosting should be fluffy and easy to spread. If too thick add a little more milk and mix.

Buttercream Frosting

1/3 cup milk

3/4 cup softened butter

2 tsp. vanilla

2 lbs. powdered sugar sifted

Prep time 12 minutes

Directions:

Beat butter, vanilla, and milk with an electric mixer until fluffy. Gradually add the sugar and mix. Frosting should be fluffy and spreadable. If too thick add a little more milk and mix.

Decorator Frosting

1 cup Crisco shortening (not butter flavored)

4 cups sifted powdered sugar

2 TBS. water

1 tsp. clear vanilla extract

1/2 tsp. clear butter flavor extract

Prep time 12 minutes

Directions:

Beat Crisco, extracts, and water with electric mixer. Gradually add sugar. Frosting should be fluffy and stiff. If too thick add a little more water or if too thin add more sugar and beat. Use for cake decorating, roses, and borders.

Desserts & More

Honie's Cheesecake

24 oz. cream cheese (3 pkg.)

3 eggs

3/4 cup sugar

3 TBS. flour

4 tsp. milk

2 tsp. lemon juice

1 tsp. vanilla extract

Zest from 1 lemon (zest is the grated peel-the yellow part only)

Temperature: Oven at 450 degrees for 10 minutes then 250 degrees for 30—35 minutes   Yield 1 8" Pie

Directions:

Soften cream cheese to room temperature. Put it in a mixing bowl and add all the rest of the ingredients. Mix with electric mixer on low to blend then on medium until completely blended. Pour into an in 8 inch spring form pan with your graham cracker crust. Make sure you spray the pan with a baking release spray (shortening and flour type). Bake as directed. Cheesecake is done when the center to is firm when tested with a toothpick. Let cool 5—10 minutes then carefully run a knife around the outside of the pie as close to the pan as possible. Carefully unlatch spring lock and let cool. Refrigerate 10 hours before serving.

Chocolate Swirl Cheesecake

Follow cheesecake recipe. Omit lemon juice and zest. Increase vanilla to 2 tsp. Increase milk to 2 TBS. Swirl 2 TBS. melted milk chocolate into the finished batter after mixing. You can use a milk chocolate bar or sweetened bakers chocolate.

Graham Cracker Crust

12—15 whole graham crackers

1/3 cup sugar

1/4 cup melted margarine

Prep time 10 minutes

Directions:

Grind crackers in a food processor or by hand until finely ground. Add the other ingredients. Press into a greased pan (spring form for cheesecake). Bake at 450 degrees for 10 minutes and cool.

Chocolate Cookie Crust

1 1/2 cups chocolate cookie crumbs

1/4 cup melted margarine

1 tsp. vanilla extract

Follow the directions for the graham cracker crust above. 30 chocolate wafers makes about 1 1/2 cups.

"Since everything is a reflection of our minds... everything can be changed by our minds." *Buddha*

Desserts & More

Brownies

1 cup butter or margarine softened

3 eggs

2 cups sugar

1 cup flour

4 squares unsweetened chocolate

1/2 tsp. salt

1 tsp. vanilla extract

1 cup walnuts

Temperature: Oven at 350 degrees for 45 minutes   Yields 24

Directions:

Melt 1/2 cup butter with the chocolate over low heat. Take 1/2 cup butter, sugar, and vanilla and beat with an electric mixer until creamy. Add eggs one at a time and beat until mixed in. Add the chocolate and mix to blend. Stir in the flour and salt until well mixed. Add the walnuts. Bake in a greased 13x9x2 pan until done.

Oatmeal Cookies

1 cup butter or margarine

1 cup brown sugar

1/2 cup white sugar

2 eggs

1 tsp. vanilla extract

3 cups old fashioned oats

1 1/2 cup flour

1/4 tsp. salt

1 tsp. baking soda

1 tsp. cinnamon

1/4 tsp. ground nutmeg

1/4 tsp. ground cloves

1 cup raisins

1 cup chopped nuts

Temperature: Oven at 350 degrees for 10—12 minutes   Yields 4 dozen

Directions:

Beat together butter, brown and white sugar, egg, water, and vanilla with an electric mixer. Beat until creamy and smooth. Sift the flour and the dry ingredients (not the oatmeal or raisins). Gradually mix into the butter sugar mixture by mixer or hand. Add the oatmeal and mix until well blended. Stir in the raisins and nuts. Drop by tablespoons onto ungreased cookie sheets. Bake until golden brown. Remove from pan and cool.

Variation:

- Add 1 cup chocolate chips
- Use cranraisins or yellow raisins
- Add 1 cup shredded coconut
- Add 1 cup butterscotch or peanut butter chips and chopped pecans

"Wisdom begins in wonder."
Socrates

Desserts & More

Chocolate Chip Cookies

2 1/4 cups flour

1 tsp. baking soda

1 tsp. salt

2 eggs

1 cup butter or margarine softened

3/4 cup sugar

3/4 cup brown sugar

1 tsp. vanilla extract

12 oz. semi-sweet chocolate chips

1 cup walnut pieces (optional)

Temperature: Oven at 375 degrees for 9—11 minutes   Makes 3—4 dozen cookies

Directions:

Mix sugars, butter, and vanilla in a bowl with an electric mixer until well blended and fluffy. Add one egg at a time mixing until well blended. Sift your dry ingredients together. Add the flour to the butter batter a little at a time mixing thoroughly. You can do this by hand if you don't have a standup mixer. Gradually add all the flour and blend well. Fold in the chocolate chips and nuts with a rubber spatula. Bake on an ungreased cookie sheet. Use a tablespoon of dough for each cookie. Bake until lightly golden brown, remove from pan, and cool.

Peanut Butter Cookies

1/2 cup smooth peanut butter

1/2 cup sugar

1/2 cup brown sugar

1/2 cup soft butter or margarine

1 egg

1 tsp. vanilla extract

1 1/4 cups flour

1/2 tsp. baking soda

1/4 tsp. salt

Temperature: Oven at 375 degrees for 10—12 minutes   Makes 3 dozen cookies

Directions:

Mix butter and peanut butter with an electric mixer until smooth and creamy. Add sugars, egg, and vanilla. Continue mixing until creamy and well blended. Sift the dry ingredients and gradually add them to the sugar mixture. Mix by hand unless you are using a large mixer.

Roll the dough by hand into 1 inch balls. Place on ungreased baking sheet and press flat with a fork making 1/4 inch thick cookies. Bake until golden brown. Remove from pan and cool.

Variation:

Drizzle with melted chocolate after baking or add 1 cup mini chocolate or peanut butter chips to batter.

"Every child is an artist. The problem is how to remain an artist once we grow up." Pablo Picasso

Desserts & More

Cake Bon Bons

Cake pieces from your favorite cake recipe

Vanilla pudding cup, vanilla buttercream frosting, or favorite jelly to moisten mixture

Optional:

Walnut pieces, mini chocolate chips, crushed oreo cookies , crushed candy, or coconut can be added to the mixture

Prep time 15 minutes

Use your cake scraps when you trim your cake tops before you frost them for this recipe...no waste ingredient!

Directions:

Crumble cake pieces or cake scraps. Add one of the ingredients listed to bind the cake together. Form into a ball and freeze. When frozen dip in melted chocolate or glaze and cool. You can also sprinkle balls with crushed nuts, sprinkles, coconut, crushed candy pieces while the chocolate is still hot right after it is dipped.

Fruit and Pudding Cups

1 pkg. each instant chocolate and vanilla pudding

1 cup whipped cream or Cool Whip

1 cup strawberry glaze or canned pie filling

Fresh berries

Shredded coconut or granola

Chocolate curls

Prep time 10 minutes   Serves 4—6

Directions:

Prepare pudding as directed on box. Put a layer of chocolate pudding in a cocktail glass. Next put a layer of berry glaze or pie filling. Add a layer of vanilla pudding. Top with a layer of whipped cream. Add cut fresh fruit on top and sprinkle with coconut, granola, or both. Top with chocolate curls. Make chocolate curls by shaving a slightly frozen chocolate candy bar with a potato peeler.

Variation:

Use pudding cups instead of boxed pudding.

Add chopped walnuts or pecans between the pudding and glaze layers.

"Patience is the companion of wisdom."   Saint Augustine

Desserts & More

Strawberry Shortcake

4 shortcake cups

4 large fresh strawberries

2 kiwi fruit or 1 mango

1/2 cup strawberry glaze

2 vanilla pudding cups

Chocolate glaze

Prep time 15 minutes   Serves 4

Directions:

Spread 1/2 pudding cup on top of the shortcake cup. Dip strawberry in glaze and place on top of pudding. Drizzle chocolate glaze over berry. Top with whipped cream if desired. Place sliced kiwi fruit or mango slices or both on sides of shortcake for color and eye appeal.

Berry Cake Delight

1 large sponge cake cup or 4 small ones

Cream Cheese Fruit Dip or vanilla pudding

Whipped cream

1 1/2 cups assorted fresh berries

Prep time 15 minutes   Serves 4

Directions:

Spread cream cheese dip or pudding across top of cake. Put a layer of whipped cream on top and then add the berries. Sprinkle chopped nuts and coconut if desired.

Fruit & Cake Cups

1 21 oz. can pie filling

1 box instant vanilla pudding

Sliced pound cake

Whipped cream

Fruits and nuts to garnish

Prep time 15 minutes   Serves 4

Directions:

Prepare pudding as directed on box. Put a slice of cake on the bottom of a glass container. Layer with pie filling, pudding, and cream. Top layer should be the pie filling. Garnish with fruits, granola, chocolate, coconut, or nuts.

Desserts & More

Basic Spa Water

2 medium lemons cut in half

2 medium limes cut in half

1 large orange cut in half

64 oz. water

Prep time 15 minutes   Yields 1/2 gallon

Directions:

Fill jug with water. Cut lemon into 6 thin slices. Cut lime into 4 thin slices and orange into 3 thin slices. Add to water. Squeeze the remaining citrus juice into the water. Chill for 4—6 hours. You can make one more batch of water when you finish the jug by adding 64 more ounces of water.

Spa Water Quencher

1 recipe basic spa water

3 leaves fresh mint crushed

4—6 thin slices peeled cucumber

Directions:

Prepare as above but add the mint and cucumber to the water. This makes a water that quenches your thirst and rehydrates you.

Spa Water Refresher

1 recipe basic spa water

6 strawberries thinly cut

1 leaf fresh mint crushed

1 extra large orange

Directions:

Prepare your basic spa water recipe. Add the juice of one additional orange and sliced strawberries. This water is a refreshing alternative to sweetened fruit drinks.

Tropical Party Punch

12 oz. frozen orange juice

12 oz. Hawaii's Own frozen Paradise Punch

8 oz. frozen limeade

1 quart tropical 100% juice blend

1 cup blended fresh watermelon

1 46 oz. can pineapple juice

2 liter ginger ale

Prep time 10 minutes   Makes 1 1/2 gallons

Directions:

Defrost frozen juices. Combine all the juices together in a large container. Freeze until slushy. Right before serving add the ginger ale. Add frozen strawberries or frozen mango slices to garnish if desired.

Desserts & More

Easy Party Fruit Punch

2 liter bottle fruit punch

1 quart orange juice

1 quart pineapple juice

1 2 liter bottle ginger ale

Sliced oranges for garnish

Prep time 10 minutes   Makes 1 1/2 gallons

Directions:

Chill juices and fruit punch well and freeze until slightly slushy. Right before serving add the ginger ale. Use sliced oranges or frozen strawberries as a garnish if desired.

Variation:

Use 64 oz. of orange juice instead of the orange and pineapple juices.

Citrus Party Punch

12 oz. can frozen orange juice

12 oz. can frozen lemonade

1 46 oz. can pineapple juice

1 cup sugar

Water to make 1 gallon

2 liters of lemon lime soda

Prep time 10 minutes   Yields 1 1/2 gallons

Directions:

Defrost the frozen juices. Put the juice, sugar, and pineapple juice into a large container. Add enough water to make 1 gallon of mix. Freeze until slushy. Right before you serve add 2 liters of lemon lime soda. You can make the punch concentrate early and freeze it. Defrost until slushy then serve with the soda.

Pink Party Punch

1 quart pineapple juice

1 quart cranberry juice

2 cups orange juice

1 1/4 cups sugar

2 liters ginger ale

1 cup frozen raspberries

Orange slices for garnish

Prep time 10 minutes   Makes 1 gallon

Directions:

Combine all the ingredients except the soda and freeze until slushy. Add the soda right before serving. You can garnish with frozen raspberries and orange slices if desired.

Flavored Iced Drink

7—8 oz. fresh brewed tea or lemonade

1 1/3 TBS . Monin Gourmet Syrup (try mango, peach, raspberry)

Ice

Directions:

Combine ingredients. This recipe makes an iced tea or lemonade that tastes like your restaurant favorite.

Index

Avocado
  Guacamole Dip, 7
Baking Candy
  Chocolate Bar, 95 98
  Choc. Chips, 96, 97
  Peanut Butter Chips, 97
Baking Tips, 2
Battering Techniques, 1
Beans
  Baked Beans, 55
  Basic Beans, 54
  Black Beans, 54
  Black Beans & Rice, 38
  Blacked Eyed Peas, 54
  Brick Chili Beans, 54
  Chili, 18
  Lentils, 55
  Lentil Soup, 52
  Mongo (Mung) Beans, 55
  Navy Bean Soup, 51
  Refried Beans, 68
  Split Pea Soup, 50
  Three Bean Salad, 80
  White Beans, 54
Bean Sprouts
  Chinese Noodle Soup, 51
  Egg Foo Yong, 59
  Pad Thai, 63
  Stir Fry, 61
  Veg. Stir Fry, 38
Beef Dishes
  Chow Mein, 60
  Corned Beef Hash, 22
  Fajitas, 41
  Stir Fry, 61
  Tacos, 46
Beef Steak
  Chicken Fried Stk., 22
  Cube Steak, 22
  Smothered Steak, 23
  Steak w/ Onions, 23
  Swiss Steak, 23
Beef Stews

Crock Pot Stew, 24
Oxtail Stew, 25
Pot Roast, 26
Shepherd Pie, 24
Stove Top Stew, 24
Bell Pepper
  Fajitas, 41
  Stir Fry, 38, 61
  Stuffed Peppers, 13
Berries
  Berry Delight, 99
  Berry Topping, 92
  Cake Filling, 92
  Fruit & Cake Cups, 99
  Fruit & Pudding Cups, 98
  Fruit Salad, 78
  Pink Party Punch, 101
  Summer Fruit Salad, 81
  Tropical Punch, 100
  Waldorf Spring Salad, 81
Bok Choy
  Chinese Noodle Soup, 51
  Stir Fry, 38,61
Breads/Crackers
  Baking Tips, 2
  Banana Nut Bread, 93
  Choc. Cookie Crust, 95
  Easy Donuts, 84
  French Toast, 85
  French Toast Pastry, 85
  Jazzed Up Pancakes, 86
  Soft Bread Crumbs, 19
  Stuffing, 66
Broccoli
  Italian Pasta Salad, 80
  Sautéed Broccoli, 71
  Stir Fry, 38,61
Cabbage
  Cabbage Rolls, 13
  Chicken Teriyaki, 62
  Chicken Soup, 50
  Chinese Noodle Soup, 51
  Cole Slaw, 81

Fried Cabbage, 70
Lumpia, 58
Pancit Bihon, 62
Stir Fry, 38, 61
Cake
  Berry Cake Delight, 99
  Cake Bob Bons, 98
  Cake Filling, 92
  Cake Frosting, 92,93,94
  Cake Pan Tips, 2
  Fruit & Cake Cups, 99
  Strawberry Shortcake, 99
Carrots
  Beef Stew, 24
  Chicken and Vegs, 44
  Chicken Casserole, 46
  Chicken Soup, 50
  Chicken Tortilla Soup, 52
  Chicken Toast, 40
  Navy Bean Soup, 51
  Oxtail Stew, 25
  Pot Roast, 26
  Shepherds Pie, 24
  Split Pea Soup, 50
  Stir Fry, 38, 61
  Tempura, 59
  Vegetarian Lasagna, 15
Casseroles
  Bean & Beef Casserole, 16
  Cheesy Tuna Casserole, 33
  Chicken Casserole, 46
  Chili Rellano Casserole, 37
  Eggplant Parmesan, 38
  Lasagna, 15
  Shepherd Pie, 24
  Taco Casserole, 14
  Tuna Casserole, 33
Cheese
  Cheddar Potato Soup, 51
  Cheese Enchilada, 37
  Cheese Omelet, 86
  Cheese Sauce, 88
  Cheesy Tuna Casserole, 33

Index

Cheese Cont.
Chili Rellano Casserole, 37
Easy Pizza, 9
Eggplant Parmesan, 38
Fun Grilled Cheese, 9
Funny Face Pizza, 10
Lasagna, 15
Stuffed Zucchini, 73
Mac & Cheese, 75, 76

Cheese, Creamed
Cream Cheese Frosting, 92
Creamy Lemon Dip, 8
Fiesta Party Dip, 7
Cheese Fruit Dip, 8
Honie's Cheesecake, 95
Nutty Cheese Ball, 8
Spicy Salsa Cheese, 6
Swirl Cheesecake, 95

Chicken Baked/Roasted
Chicken & Vegs, 44
Honie's Hot Wings, 6
Oven BBQ Chicken, 40
Roasted Chicken, 46
Stuffed Chicken Breast, 44

Chicken Dishes
Adobo, 63
Chicken Casserole, 46
Chicken Chow Mein, 60
Chicken Salad, 79
Chicken Soup, 50
Chicken Tacos, 46
Chicken Teriyaki, 62
Chicken Tortilla Soup, 52
Fajitas, 41
Fried Chicken, 47
Pad Thai, 63
Shredded Chicken, 46
Stir Fry, 61

Chicken in Sauce
Chicken Cacciatori, 42
Chicken in Green Sauce, 46
Chicken Toast, 40
Smothered Chicken, 48

Chilies
Chili Rellano, 36
Chili Rellano Casserole, 37
Fiesta Party Dip, 7
Huevos Rancheros, 84
Salsa, 7

Citrus
Fruit Salad, 78
Shrimp Salad, 79
Spa Water, Citrus, 100
Summer Fruit Salad, 81
Waldorf Spring Salad, 81

Cookies
Brownies, 96
Chocolate Chip, 97
Oatmeal, 96
Peanut Butter, 97

Crusts
Graham Cracker, 95
Chocolate Cookie, 95

Cucumber
Cucumber Salad, 78

Donuts
Easy Donuts, 84

Dried Fruit
Coconut, 96
Cranraisins, 81, 96
Raisins, 93, 96

Eggs
Breakfast Potato Hash, 86
Croquettes, 34
Egg Foo Yong, 59
Egg Wash, 1
Folding Eggs, 88
Huevos Rancheros, 84
Omelet, 86
Spanish Tortilla Pie, 18
Tempura Batter, 59

Eggplant
Eggplant Parmesan, 38
Sautéed, 71
Vegetarian Lasagna, 15

Fillings

Cake Filling, 92
Pie Filling, 98, 99

Fish
Baked Fish, 32
Baked Salmon, 32
Cheesy Tuna Casserole, 33
Croquettes, 34
Fried Fish, 32
Italian Baked Fish, 32
Pan Fried Fish, 32
Tuna Casserole, 33

Frosting
Buttercream Frosting, 94
Cream Cheese Frosting, 92
Decorator Frosting, 94
Easy Glazes, 94
Fudge Frosting, 94
Whip Cream Frosting, 93
Whipped Decorator, 93

Fruits
Banana Nut Bread, 93
Berry Cake Delight, 99
Berry Topping, 92
Creamy Lemon Dip, 8
Fruit & Cake Cups, 99
Fruit & Pudding Cups, 98
Fruit Salad, 78
Peanut Butter Treats, 9
Strawberry Shortcake, 99
Summer Fruit Salad, 81
Waldorf Spring Salad, 81

Greens
Greens, 72

Green Beans
Been & Beef Casserole, 16
Beef Stew, 24
Pot Roast, 26
Shepherds Pie, 24

Ground Beef/Turkey
BBQ Mac, 17
Bean & Beef Casserole, 16
Cabbage Rolls, 13
Chili Mac, 17

Index

Ground Beef/Turkey cont.
 Chili with Beans, 18
 Easy Beefy Noodles, 16
 Lasagna, 15
 Lumpia, 58
 Meatloaf, 19
 Mexican Mac, 17
 Spaghetti Sauce, 14
 Spanish Tortilla Pie, 18
 Stuffed Peppers, 13
 Substitution Tips, 3
 Taco Casserole, 14
 Tacos, 46
 Tin Nok Tok, 12
 Zucchini & Meatballs, 12
Ham
 Black Eyed Peas, 54
 Beans, 54
 Glazed Baked Ham, 28
 Green Beans, 71
 Greens, 72
 Ham Salad, 79
 Sliced Ham, 28
 Soups, 50, 51, 52
Hens
 Cornish Game Hen, 43
Kid's Meals
 Easy Kid's Pizza, 9
 Fun Grilled Cheese, 9
 Funny Face Pizza, 10
 Kids Morning Treat, 10
 Peanut Butter Treats, 9
 Pizza Face Wedge, 10
Lettuce
 Lentils, 55
 Summer Fruit & Salad, 81
 Waldorf Spring Salad, 81
Mushrooms
 Chinese Noodle Soup, 51
 Lumpia, 58
 Omelet, 86
 Shrimp in Wine Sauce, 33
 Smothered Chicken, 48

Smothered Steak, 23
Spaghetti Sauce, 14
Steak & Onions, 23
Stir Fry, 38, 61
Swiss Steak, 23
Tempura, 59
Okra
 Sautéed, 71
Pasta
 BBQ Mac, 17
 Cheesy Tuna Casserole, 33
 Chicken Casserole, 46
 Chili Mac, 17
 Chinese Noodle Soup, 51
 Chow Mein, 60
 Easy Beefy Noodles, 16
 Italian Pasta Salad, 80
 Lasagna, 15
 macaroni & cheese, 75,76
 Mexican Style Mac, 17
 Pad Thai, 63
 Pancit Bihon, 62
 Pasta Salad, 79
 Seafood Pasta Salad, 80
 Spaghetti, 14
 Three Bean Salad, 80
Peas
 Chicken Toast, 40
 Oxtail Stew, 25
 Shepherd Pie, 24
 Stews, 24
 Tuna casseroles, 33
Pie Crusts
 Chocolate Crust, 95
 Graham Crust, 95
Pork
 Adobo, 63
 Breaded Pork Chops, 29
 Breakfast Potato Hash, 86
 Country Style Ribs, 28
 Pork Chops, 29
 Pork Fried Rice, 67
Potatoes

Casseroles, 16,24,46
Chicken & Vegetables, 44
Hash with Meat, 22,86
Home Fried Potatoes, 69
Lumpia, 58
Omelet, 86
Pot Roast, 26
Potato Patties, 69
Potato Salad, 74
Scalloped Potatoes, 68
Spanish Tortilla Pie, 18
Soups, 50, 51
Stews, 24, 25
Tin Nok Tok, 12
Twice Baked Potatoes, 70
Punch
 Tropical Party Punch, 100
 Easy Party Punch, 101
 Citrus Party Punch, 101
 Pink Party Punch, 101
Raisins,
 Peanut Butter Treats, 9
 Banana Nut Bread, 93
 Oatmeal Cookies, 96
 Salads, 81
Rice
 Black Beans and Rice, 38
 fried, 67
 Hen Stuffing, 43
 Peppers, Stuffed, 13
 Spanish Rice, 67
Sauces
 Asian Marinade, 89
 BBQ Sauce, 89
 Cheese Sauce, 88
 Fish Marinade, 89
 Gravy, 59, 88
 White Sauce, 88
Shrimp
 Noodles, Asian, 60, 62, 63
 Egg Foo Yong, 59
 Fried Rice, 67
 Fajitas, 41

Index

Shrimp Continued
 Fried Shrimp, 32
 Lumpia, 58
 Seafood Pasta Salad, 80
 Shrimp in Wine Sauce, 33
 Shrimp Salad, 79
 Stir Fry, 61
 Tempura, 59
Soda
 Party Punches, 100, 101
Spa Water
 Basic Spa Water, 100
 Spa Water Quencher, 100
 Spa Water Refresher, 100
Spices
 Seasoning Tips, 1
 Spice List, 2
Spinach
 Mongo Beans, 55
 Salads, 81
 Spanish Tortilla Pie, 18
 Chicken Breast, Stuffed, 44
 Vegetarian Lasagna, 15
Squash
 Sautéed, 71, 76
Stir Fry
 Basic Stir Fry, 61
 Vegetable Stir Fry, 38
Tea
 Flavored Iced Tea, 101
Tips & Hints
 Baking, 2
 Battering, 1
 Cooking, 3
 Folding Whipped Eggs, 88
 Folding Eggrolls, 58
 Ground Meat Substitute, 3
 Marinating, 1
 Seasoning, 1
 Spices, 2
Tomatoes, Fresh
 Asian Noodles, 60, 62
 Baked Fish, 32

Chicken Tortilla Soup, 52
Fried Green Tomatoes, 68
Navy Bean Soup, 51
Omelet, 86
Salad, 81
Salsa, 7
Sauce, Ranchero, 84
Sautéed Zucchini, 71
Stuffed Zucchini, 73
White Beans, 54
Tomatoes, Canned
 Chicken Cacciatore, 42
 Chili Mac, 17
 Chili with Beans, 18
 Oxtail Stew, 25
 Best Salsa, 7
 Spaghetti Sauce, 14
 Spanish Rice, 67
 Swiss Steak, 23
Turkey
 Roasted Turkey, 45
 Smothered Turkey Wings, 41
 Turkey Soup, 50
Turnips
 Turnips and Greens, 72
Water
 Citrus Spa Waters, 100
Yams
 Chicken & Vegetables, 44
 Candied Yams, 73
 Pot Roast, 26
 Stews, 24
 Whipped, 74
Zucchini
 Chicken Soup, 50
 Greek Vegetables, 76
 Lasagna, 15
 Sautéed Zucchini, 71
 Stir Fry, 38
 Stuffed Zucchini, 73
 Tempura, 59

About the Author

Linda Hayes was born in Southern California to first generation immigrants from the Philippines. She grew up in the Philippines and returned to her place of birth, the United States, to attend college. She is the youngest of four, a mother of five children and a grandmother.

Her career path has been mother, businesswoman, educator, trainer, author, and speaker. Her book, The Voice Hidden Within Me—A Journey of Discovery and Healing Your Heart was released in January of 2013. This inspirational true life story about struggle, overcoming obstacles, and success was the first book in her Heart Chatter series.

Simply Tasty—-Easy Meals on a Budget is her next work. •Although it is a cookbook it follows her same pattern of inspiring others by including inspiring words and quotes throughout the cookbook.

Hayes learned how to cook as a young preteen living in the Philippines. Cooking became her hobby since there was no interference from television in her small home town. Her cooking style was developed by learning scratch cooking and generational recipes from her mother. The cookbooks she read daily as a youth became her novels. Instead of following recipes step by step she took the "idea" of the recipes experimenting until she made a recipe she liked.

Her basic cooking skills have been enhanced by incorporating international foods she learned to cook over the years. Her traveling and living in numerous multicultural environments has influenced her cooking style. In addition cooking for five children as a single mother gave her insight on how to make tasty, easy, and cost effective meals. Her motto is "Use what you have on hand, be creative, it is okay to substitute!"

Visit her author page on: www.HeartChatter.com and www.Publishing-USA.com

www.ingramcontent.com/pod-product-compliance
Lightning Source LLC
Chambersburg PA
CBHW081542040426
42448CB00015B/3191